GREEK GODS & GODDESSES

GREEK GODS & GODDESSES

EDITED BY MICHAEL TAFT

Britannica
Educational Publishing

IN ASSOCIATION WITH

ROSEN
EDUCATIONAL SERVICES

Published in 2014 by Britannica Educational Publishing (a trademark of Encyclopædia
Britannica, Inc.) in association with The Rosen Publishing Group, Inc.
29 East 21st Street, New York, NY 10010

Distributed exclusively by Rosen Publishing.
To see additional Britannica Educational Publishing titles, go to http://
www.rosenpublishing.com

First Edition

Britannica Educational Publishing
J. E. Luebering: Director, Core Reference Group
Anthony L. Green: Editor, Compton's by Britannica

Rosen Publishing
Hope Lourie Killcoyne: Executive Editor
Michael Taft: Editor
Nelson Sá: Art Director
Brian Garvey: Designer
Cindy Reiman: Photography Manager
Nicole Baker: Photo Researcher

Cataloging-in-Publication Data

Greek gods & goddesses/edited by Michael Taft.—First Edition.
   pages cm.—(Gods & goddesses of mythology)
"In association with Britannica Educational Publishing, Rosen Educational Services."
Includes bibliographical references and index.
ISBN 978-1-62275-152-5 (library binding)
1. Gods, Greek. 2. Goddesses, Greek. 3. Mythology, Greek. I. Taft, Michael W., editor of
compilation. II. Title: Greek gods and goddesses.
BL783.G68 2013
292.2'11—dc23

2013021955

Manufactured in the Malaysia

Cover: Statue of Pallas Athena at the Austrian Parliament in Vienna. *jorisvo/Shutterstock.com*

CONTENTS

Introduction   8

Chapter 1: Forms of Myth in Greek Culture   13

Chapter 2: Types of Myths in Greek Culture   16

Chapter 3: Greek Mythological Characters and Motifs in Art and Literature   25

Chapter 4: Gods and Goddesses   27

- Aphrodite   27
- Apollo   30
- Ares   34
- Artemis   36
- Asclepius   39
- Athena   41
- Atlas   45
- Calliope   48
- Clio   49
- Cronus   50
- Demeter   53
- Dionysus   57
- Eos   61
- Eros   63
- Euterpe   65
- Gaea   66
- Hades   68
- Hebe   71
- Hephaestus   72
- Hera   73
- Heracles   75

- Hermes — 78
- Hestia — 81
- Hygieia — 82
- Hypnos — 84
- Melpomene — 85
- Mnemosyne — 86
- Morpheus — 87
- Nemesis — 88
- Nike — 89
- Nyx — 91
- Oceanus — 92
- Pan — 93
- Persephone — 98
- Phoebe — 100
- Polyhymnia — 102
- Poseidon — 103
- Prometheus — 106
- Rhea — 108
- Selene — 109
- Terpsichore — 110
- Thalia — 111
- Thanatos — 112
- Themis — 114
- Tyche — 116
- Urania — 117
- Uranus — 118
- Zeus — 120

Glossary — 123
For Further Reading — 125
Index — 127

INTRODUCTION

Illustration representing the 12 Olympians: Zeus, Hera, Poseidon, Demeter, Athena, Hestia, Apollo, Artemis, Ares, Aphrodite, Hephaestus, and Hermes. Leemage/Universal Images Group/Getty Images

G reek mythology is the body of stories concerning the gods, heroes, and rituals of the ancient Greeks. That the myths contained a considerable element of fiction was recognized by the more critical Greeks, such as the philosopher Plato in the 5th–4th centuries BCE. In general, however, in the popular piety of the Greeks, the myths were viewed as true accounts. Greek mythology has subsequently had extensive influence on the arts and literature of Western civilization, which fell heir to much of Greek culture.

Although people of all countries, eras, and stages of civilization have developed myths that explain the existence and workings of natural phenomena, recount the deeds of gods or heroes, or seek to justify social or political institutions, the myths of the Greeks have remained unrivaled in the Western world as sources of imaginative and appealing ideas. Poets and artists from ancient times to the present have derived inspiration from Greek mythology and have discovered contemporary significance and relevance in Classical mythological themes.

THE HOMERIC POEMS: THE *ILIAD* AND THE *ODYSSEY*

The 5th-century-BCE Greek historian Herodotus remarked that the Greek poets Homer and Hesiod gave to the Olympian gods their familiar characteristics. Few today would accept this literally. In the first book of the *Iliad*, the son of Zeus and Leto (Apollo, line 9) is as instantly identifiable to the Greek reader by his patronymic as are the sons of Atreus (Agamemnon and Menelaus, line 16). In both cases, the audience is expected to have knowledge of the myths that preceded their literary rendering. Little is known to suggest that the Greeks treated Homer, or any other source of Greek myths, as mere entertainment, whereas there are prominent Greeks from Pindar to the later Stoa for whom myths, and those from Homer in particular, are so serious as to warrant bowdlerization or allegorization.

THE WORKS OF HESIOD: *THEOGONY* AND *WORKS AND DAYS*

The fullest and most important source of myths about the origin of the gods is the *Theogony* of Hesiod (c. 700 BCE). The elaborate genealogies are accompanied by folktales and etiological myths. The *Works and Days* shares some of these in the context of a farmer's calendar and an extensive harangue on the subject of justice addressed to Hesiod's possibly fictitious brother Perses. The orthodox view treats the two poems as quite different in theme and treats the *Works and Days* as a theodicy (a natural theology). It is possible, however, to treat the two poems as a diptych, each part dependent on the other. The *Theogony* declares the identities and alliances of the gods, while the *Works and Days* gives advice on the best way to succeed in a dangerous world; and Hesiod urges that the most reliable—though by no means certain—way is to be just.

OTHER LITERARY WORKS

Fragmentary post-Homeric epics of varying date and authorship filled the gaps in the accounts of the Trojan War recorded in the *Iliad* and *Odyssey*; the so-called Homeric Hymns (shorter surviving poems) are the source of several important religious myths. Many of the lyric poets preserved various myths, but the odes of Pindar of Thebes (flourished 6th–5th century BCE) are particularly rich in myth and legend. The works of the three tragedians—Aeschylus, Sophocles, and Euripides, all of the 5th century BCE—are remarkable for the variety of the traditions they preserve.

In Hellenistic times (323–30 BCE) Callimachus, a 3rd-century-BCE poet and scholar in Alexandria, recorded many obscure myths; one of his contemporaries, the mythographer Euhemerus, suggested that the gods were originally human, a view known as Euhemerism. Apollonius of Rhodes, another scholar of the 3rd century BCE, preserved the fullest account of the Argonauts in search of the Golden Fleece.

In the period of the Roman Empire, the *Geography* of Strabo (1st century BCE), the *Library* of the pseudo-Apollodorus (attributed to a 2nd-century-AD scholar), the antiquarian writings of the Greek biographer Plutarch, and the works of Pausanias, a 2nd-century-AD historian, as well as the *Latin Genealogies* of Hyginus, a 2nd-century-AD mythographer, have provided valuable sources in Latin of later Greek mythology.

ARCHAEOLOGICAL DISCOVERIES

The discovery of the Mycenaean civilization by Heinrich Schliemann, a 19th-century German amateur archaeologist, and the discovery of the Minoan civilization in Crete (from which the Mycenaean ultimately derived) by Sir Arthur Evans, a 20th-century English archaeologist, are essential to the 21st-century understanding of the development of myth and ritual in the Greek world. Such discoveries illuminated aspects of Minoan culture from about 2200 to 1450 BCE and Mycenaean culture from about 1600 to 1200 BCE; these eras were followed by a Dark Age that lasted until about 800 BCE. Unfortunately, the evidence about myth and ritual at Mycenaean and Minoan sites is entirely monumental because the Linear B script (an ancient form of Greek found in both Crete and Greece) was mainly used to record inventories.

Geometric designs on pottery of the 8th century BCE depict scenes from the Trojan cycle, as well as the adventures of Heracles. The extreme formality of the style, however, renders much of the identification difficult, and there is no inscriptional evidence accompanying the designs to assist scholars in identification and interpretation. In the succeeding Archaic (c. 750–c. 500 BCE), Classical (c. 480–323 BCE), and Hellenistic periods, Homeric and various other mythological scenes appear to supplement the existing literary evidence.

FORMS OF MYTH IN GREEK CULTURE

CHAPTER 1

To distinguish between myth, legend, and folktale can be useful, provided it is remembered that the Greeks themselves did not do so.

RELIGIOUS MYTHS

Greek religious myths are concerned with gods or heroes in their more serious aspects or are connected with ritual. They include cosmogonical tales of the genesis of the gods and the world out of Chaos, the successions of divine rulers, and the internecine struggles that culminated in the supremacy of Zeus, the ruling god of Olympus (the mountain that was considered the home of the gods). They also include the long tale of Zeus's amours with goddesses and mortal women, which usually resulted in the births of younger deities and heroes. The goddess Athena's unique status is implicit in the story of her motherless birth (she sprang full grown from Zeus's forehead); and the myths of Apollo explain that god's sacral associations, describe his remarkable victories over monsters and giants, and stress his jealousy and the dangers inherent in immortal alliances.

Myths of Dionysus, on the other hand, demonstrate the hostility aroused by a novel faith. Some myths are closely associated with rituals, such as the account of the drowning of the infant Zeus's cries by the Curetes, attendants of Zeus, clashing their weapons, or Hera's annual restoration of her virginity by bathing in the spring Canathus. Some myths about heroes and heroines also have a religious basis. The tale of creation and moral decline forms part of the myth of the Four Ages. The subsequent destruction of humanity by flood and regeneration of humans from stones is partly based on folktale.

LEGENDS

Myths were viewed as embodying divine or timeless truths, whereas legends (or sagas) were quasi-historical. Hence, famous events in epics, such as the Trojan War, were generally regarded as having really happened, and heroes and heroines were believed to have actually lived. Earlier sagas, such as the voyage of the Argonauts, were accepted in a similar fashion. Most Greek legends were embellished with folktales and fiction, but some certainly contain a historical substratum. Such are the tales of more than one sack of Troy, which are supported by archaeological evidence, and the labours of Heracles, which might suggest Mycenaean feudalism. Again, the legend of the Minotaur (a being part human, part bull) could have arisen from exaggerated accounts of bull leaping in ancient Crete.

In another class of legends, heinous offenses—such as attempting to rape a goddess, deceiving the gods grossly by inculpating them in crime, or assuming their prerogatives—were punished by everlasting torture in the underworld. The consequences of social crimes, such as murder or incest, were also described in legend (e.g., the story of Oedipus, who killed his father and married his mother). Legends were also sometimes employed to justify existing political systems or to bolster territorial claims.

FOLKTALES

Folktales, consisting of popular recurring themes and told for amusement, inevitably found their way into Greek myth. Such is the theme of lost persons—whether husband, wife, or child (e.g., Odysseus, Helen of Troy, or Paris of Troy)—found or recovered after long and exciting adventures. Journeys to the land of the dead were made by Orpheus (a hero who went to Hades to restore his dead wife, Eurydice, to the realm of the living), Heracles, Odysseus, and Theseus (the slayer of the Minotaur). The victory of the little man by means of cunning against impossible odds, the exploits of the superman (e.g., Heracles), or the long-delayed victory over enemies are still as popular with modern writers as they were with the Greeks.

The successful countering of the machinations of cruel sires and stepmothers, the rescue of princesses from monsters, and temporary forgetfulness at a crucial moment are also familiar themes in Greek myth. Recognition by tokens, such as peculiarities of dress or Odysseus's scar, is another common folktale motif. The babes-in-the-woods theme of the exposure of children and their subsequent recovery is also found in Greek myth. The Greeks, however, also knew of the exposure of children as a common practice.

CHAPTER 2

TYPES OF MYTHS IN GREEK CULTURE

In Greek culture, myths (especially myths of origin) represent an attempt to render the universe comprehensible in human terms. Greek creation myths (cosmogonies) and views of the universe (cosmologies) were more systematic and specific than those of other ancient peoples. Yet their very artistry serves as an impediment to interpretation, since the Greeks embellished the myths with folktale and fiction told for its own sake. Thus, though the aim of Hesiod's *Theogony* is to describe the ascendancy of Zeus (and, incidentally, the rise of the other gods), the inclusion of such familiar themes as the hostility between the generations, the enigma of woman (Pandora), the exploits of the friendly trickster (Prometheus), and the struggles against powerful beings or monsters like the Titans (and, in later tradition, the Giants) enhances the interest of an epic account.

According to Hesiod, four primary divine beings first came into existence: the Gap (Chaos), Earth (Gaea), the Abyss (Tartarus), and Love (Eros). The creative process began with the forcible separation of Gaea from her doting consort Heaven (Uranus) in order to allow her progeny to be born. The means of separation employed, the cutting off of Uranus's genitals by his son Cronus, bears a certain resemblance to a similar story recorded in Babylonian epic. The crudity is relieved, however, in characteristic Greek fashion, by the friendly collaboration of Uranus and Gaea, after their divorce, on a plan to save Zeus from the same Cronus, his cannibalistic sire.

Relief sculpture of Helios in his chariot, located in the Berlin State Museums.
Staatliche Museen zu Berlin-Preussischer Kulturbesitz

According to Greek cosmological concepts, the Earth was viewed as a flat disk afloat on the river of Ocean. The Sun (Helios) traversed the heavens like a charioteer and sailed around the Earth in a golden bowl at night. Natural fissures were popularly regarded as entrances to the subterranean house of Hades, i.e., the home of the dead.

MYTHS OF THE AGES OF THE WORLD

From a very early period, Greek myths seem to have been open to criticism and alteration on grounds of morality or of misrepresentation of known facts. In the *Works and Days*, Hesiod makes use of a scheme of Four Ages (or Races): Golden, Silver, Bronze, and Iron. "Race" is the more accurate translation, but "Golden Age" has become so established in English that both terms should be mentioned. These races or ages are separate creations of the gods, the Golden Age belonging to the reign of Cronus and the subsequent races being the creation of Zeus. Those of the Golden Age never grew old, were free from toil, and passed their time in jollity and feasting. When they died, they became guardian spirits on Earth.

Why the Golden Age came to an end Hesiod failed to explain, but it was succeeded by the Silver Age. After an inordinately prolonged childhood, the men of the Silver Age began to act presumptuously and neglected the gods. Consequently, Zeus hid them in the Earth, where they became spirits among the dead.

Zeus next created the men of the Bronze Age, men of violence who perished by mutual destruction. At this point the poet intercalates the Age (or Race) of Heroes. He thereby destroys the symmetry of the myth, in the interests of history: what is now known as the Minoan-Mycenaean period was generally believed in antiquity to have been a good time to live. (This subjection of myth to history is not universal in Greece, but it is found in writers such as Hesiod, Xenophanes, Pindar, Aeschylus, and Plato.) Of these heroes the more-favoured (who were related to the gods) reverted to a kind of restored Golden Age existence under the rule of Cronus (forced into honourable exile by his son Zeus) in the Isles of the Blessed.

The final age, the antithesis of the Golden Age, was the Iron Age, during which the poet himself had the misfortune to live. But even that was not the worst, for he believed that a time would come when infants would be born old and there would be no recourse left against the universal moral decline. The presence of evil was explained by Pandora's rash action in opening the fatal jar.

Elsewhere in Greek and Roman literature, the belief in successive periods or races is found with the belief that by some means, when the worst is reached, the system gradually (Plato, *Politikos*) or quickly (Virgil, *Fourth Eclogue*) returns to the Golden Age. Hesiod may have known this version; he wishes to have been born either earlier or later. There is also a myth of progress, associated with Prometheus, god of craftsmen, but the progress is limited, for the 19th-century concept of eternal advancement is absent from Greek thought.

MYTHS OF THE GODS

Myths about the gods described their births, victories over monsters or rivals, love affairs, special powers, or connections with a cultic site or ritual. As these powers tended to be wide, the myths of many gods were correspondingly complex. Thus, the Homeric Hymns to Demeter, a goddess of agriculture, and to the Delian and Pythian Apollo describe how these deities came to be associated with sites at Eleusis, Delos, and Delphi, respectively. Similarly, myths about Athena, the patroness of Athens, tend to emphasize the goddess's love of war and her affection for heroes and the city of Athens; and those concerning Hermes (the messenger of the gods), Aphrodite (goddess of love), or Dionysus describe Hermes' proclivities as a god of thieves, Aphrodite's lovemaking, and Dionysus's association with wine, frenzy, miracles, and even ritual death. Poseidon (god of the sea) was unusually atavistic in that his union with Earth and his equine adventures appear to hark back to his premarine status as a horse or earthquake god.

Many myths are treated as trivial and lighthearted; but this judgment rests on the suppressed premise that any divine behaviour that seems inappropriate for a major religion must have seemed absurd and fictitious to the Greeks. Homer barely mentions the judgment of Paris, but he knew the far from trivial consequences for Troy of the favour of Aphrodite and the bitter enmity of Hera and Athena, which the "judgment of Paris" was composed to explain.

As time went on, an accretion of minor myths continued to supplement the older and more authentic ones. Thus, the loves of Apollo, virtually ignored by Homer and Hesiod, explained why the bay (or laurel) became Apollo's sacred tree and how he came to father Asclepius, a healing god. Similarly, the presence of the cuckoo on Hera's sceptre at Hermione or the invention of the panpipe were explained by fables. Such etiological myths proliferated during the Hellenistic era, though in the earlier periods genuine examples are harder to detect.

Of folk deities, the nymphs (nature goddesses) personified nature or the life in water or trees and were said to punish unfaithful lovers. Water nymphs (Naiads) were reputed to drown those with whom they fell in love, such as Hylas, a companion of Heracles. Even the gentle Muses (goddesses of the arts and sciences) blinded their human rivals, such as the bard Thamyris. Satyrs (youthful folk deities with bestial features) and sileni (old and drunken folk deities) were the nymphs' male counterparts. Like sea deities, sileni possessed secret knowledge that they would reveal only under duress. Charon, the grisly ferryman of the dead, was also a popular figure of folktale.

Myths of Heroes

Hero myths included elements from tradition, folktale, and fiction. The saga of the Argonauts, for example, is highly complex and includes elements from folktale and fiction. Episodes in the Trojan cycle, such as the departure of the Greek fleet from Aulis or Theseus's Cretan expedition and death on Scyros, may belong to traditions dating from the Minoan-Mycenaean world. On the other hand, events described in the *Iliad* probably owe far more to Homer's creative ability than to genuine tradition. Even heroes like Achilles, Hector, or Diomedes are largely fictional, though doubtlessly based on legendary prototypes. The *Odyssey* is the prime example of the wholesale importation of folktales into epic. All the best-known Greek hero myths, such as the labours of Heracles and the adventures of Perseus, Cadmus, Pelops, or Oedipus, depend more for their interest on folktales than on legend.

Certain heroes—Heracles, the Dioscuri (the twins Castor and Pollux), Amphiaraus (one of the Argonauts), and Hyacinthus (a youth whom Apollo loved and accidentally killed)—may be regarded as partly legend and partly religious myth. Thus, whereas Heracles, a man of Tiryns, may originally have been a historical character, the myth of his demise on Oeta and subsequent elevation to full divinity is closely linked with a cult. In time, Heracles' popularity was responsible for connecting his story with the Argonauts, an earlier attack on Troy, and with Theban myth. Similarly, the exploits of the Dioscuri are those of typical heroes: fighting, carrying off women, and cattle rustling. After their death they passed six months alternately beneath the Earth and in the world above, which suggests that their worship, like that of Persephone (the daughter of Zeus and Demeter), was connected with fertility or seasonal change.

MYTHS OF SEASONAL RENEWAL

Certain myths, in which goddesses or heroes were temporarily incarcerated in the underworld, were allegories of seasonal renewal. Perhaps the best-known myth of this type is the one that tells how Hades, the god of the underworld, carried Persephone off to be his consort, causing her mother, Demeter, the goddess of grain, to allow the earth to grow barren out of her grief. Because of her mother's grief, Zeus permitted Persephone to spend four months of the year in the house of Hades and eight in the light of day. In less benign climates, she was said to spend six months of the year in each. Some scholars hold that Persephone's time below ground represents the summer months, when Greek fields are parched and bare; but the Hymn to Demeter, the earliest source for the myth, states explicitly that Persephone returns when the spring flowers are flourishing (line 401). Myths of seasonal renewal, in which the deity dies and returns to life at particular times of the year, are plentiful. An important Greek example is the Cretan Zeus, mentioned previously.

Myths Involving Animal Transformations

Many Greek myths involve animal transformations, though there is no proof that theriolatry (animal worship) was ever practiced by the Greeks. Gods sometimes assumed the form of beasts in order to deceive goddesses or women. Zeus, for example, assumed the form of a bull when he carried off Europa, a Phoenician princess, and he appeared in the guise of a swan in order to attract Leda, wife of a king of Sparta. Poseidon took the shape of a stallion to beget the wonder horses Arion and Pegasus.

These myths do not suggest theriolatry. No worship is offered to the deity concerned. The animals serve other purposes in the narratives. Bulls were the most powerful animals known to the Greeks and may have been worshipped in the remote past. But, for the Greeks, in even the earliest sources there is no indication that Zeus or Poseidon were once bulls or horses or that Hera was ever

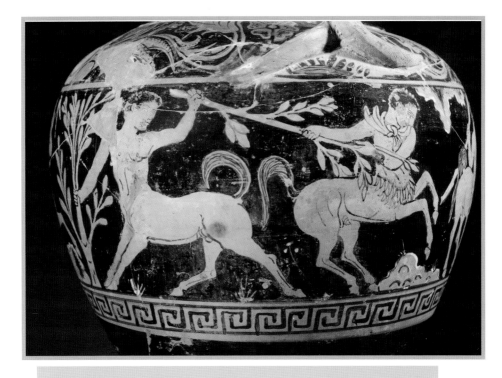

A 4th-century-BCE Etruscan amphora, or container, from Porano, Umbria, Italy, depicting a battle between centaurs. DEA/G.Nimatallah/De Agostini/Getty Images

"ox-eyed" other than metaphorically or that "gray-eyed" Athena was ever "owl-faced."

OTHER TYPES

Other types of myth exemplified the belief that the gods sometimes appeared on Earth disguised as men and women and rewarded any help or hospitality offered them. Baucis, an old Phrygian woman, and Philemon, her husband, for example, were saved from a flood by offering hospitality to Zeus and Hermes, both of whom were in human form.

The punishment of mortals' presumption in claiming to be the gods' superiors, whether in musical skill or even the number of their children, is described in several myths. The gods' jealousy of mortals' musical talents appears in the beating and flaying of the aulos-playing satyr, Marsyas, by Athena and Apollo, as well as in the attaching of ass's ears to King Midas for failing to appreciate the superiority of Apollo's music to that of the god Pan. Jealousy was the motive for the slaying of Niobe's many children because Niobe flaunted her fecundity to the goddess Leto, who had only two offspring. Similar to such stories are the moral tales about the fate of Icarus, who flew too high on home-made wings, or the myth about Phaethon, the son of Helios, who failed to perform a task too great for him (controlling the horses of the chariot of the Sun).

Transformation into a flower or tree—whether to escape a god's embrace (as with Daphne, a nymph transformed into a laurel tree), as the result of an accident (as with Hyacinthus, a friend of Apollo, who was changed into a flower), or because of pride (as with the beautiful youth Narcissus, who fell in love with his own reflection and was changed into a flower)—was a familiar theme in Greek myth.

Also popular were myths of fairylands, such as the Garden of the Hesperides (in the far west) or the land of the Hyperboreans (in the far north), or encounters with unusual creatures, such as the Centaurs, or distinctive societies, such as the Amazons.

Greek Mythological Characters and Motifs in Art and Literature

Western people of all eras have been moved and baffled by the deceptive simplicity of Greek myths, and Greek mythology has had a profound effect on the development of Western civilization.

The earliest visual representations of mythological characters and motifs occur in late Mycenaean and sub-Mycenaean art. Though identification is controversial Centaurs, a siren, and even Zeus's lover Europa have been recognized. Mythological and epic themes are also found in Geometric art of the 8th century BCE, but not until the 7th century did such themes become popular in both ceramic and sculptured works. During the Classical and subsequent periods, they became commonplace. The birth of Athena was the subject of the east pediment of the Parthenon in Athens, and the legend of Pelops and of the labours of Heracles were the subjects of the corresponding pediment and the metopes (a space on a Doric frieze) of the Temple of Zeus at Olympia. The battles of gods with Giants and of Lapiths (a wild race in northern Greece) with Centaurs were also favourite motifs. Pompeian frescoes reveal realistic representations of Theseus and Ariadne, Perseus, the fall of Icarus, and the death of Pyramus.

The great Renaissance masters added a new dimension to Greek mythology. Among the best-known subjects of Italian artists are Sandro Botticelli's *Birth of Venus*, the Ledas of Leonardo da Vinci and Michelangelo, and Raphael's *Galatea*.

Through the medium of Latin and, above all, the works of Ovid, Greek myth influenced poets such as Dante and Petrarch in Italy and Geoffrey Chaucer in England and, later, the English Elizabethans and John Milton. Jean Racine in France and Johann Wolfgang von Goethe in Germany revived Greek drama, and nearly all the major English poets from William Shakespeare to Robert Bridges turned for inspiration to Greek mythology. In later centuries, Classical themes were reinterpreted by such major dramatists as Jean Anouilh, Jean Cocteau, and Jean Giraudoux in France; Eugene O'Neill in America; and T.S. Eliot in England and by great novelists such as James Joyce (Irish) and André Gide (French). The German composers Christoph Gluck (18th century) and Richard Strauss (20th century), the German-French composer Jacques Offenbach (19th century), the Russian composer Igor Stravinsky (20th century), and many others have set Greek mythological themes to music.

GODS AND GODDESSES  CHAPTER 4

APHRODITE

A phrodite was the ancient Greek goddess of sexual love and beauty, identified with Venus by the Romans. The Greek word *aphros* means "foam," and Hesiod relates in his *Theogony* that Aphrodite was born from the white foam produced by the severed genitals of Uranus (Heaven), after his son Cronus threw them into the sea. Aphrodite was, in fact, widely worshipped as a goddess of the sea and of seafaring; she was also honoured as a goddess of war, especially at Sparta, Thebes, Cyprus, and other places. However, she was known primarily as a goddess of love and fertility and even occasionally presided over marriage. Although prostitutes considered Aphrodite their patron, her public cult was generally solemn and even austere.

Many scholars believe Aphrodite's worship came to Greece from the East, and many of her characteristics must be considered Semitic. Although Homer called her "Cyprian" after the island chiefly famed for her worship, she was already Hellenized by the time of Homer, and, according to Homer, she was the daughter of Zeus and Dione, his consort at Dodona. In Book 8 of the *Odyssey*, Aphrodite was mismatched with Hephaestus, the lame smith god, and she consequently spent her time philandering with the handsome god of war, Ares (by whom she became the mother of Harmonia, the warrior twins Phobos and Deimos, and Eros, the god of love).

A fresco in Pompeii depicting the goddess Aphrodite. iStockphoto/ Thinkstock

Of Aphrodite's mortal lovers, the most important were the Trojan shepherd Anchises, by whom she became the mother of Aeneas, and the handsome youth Adonis (in origin a Semitic nature deity and the consort of Ishtar-Astarte), who was killed by a boar while hunting and was lamented by women at the festival of Adonia. The cult of Adonis had underworld features, and Aphrodite was also connected with the dead at Delphi.

Aphrodite's main centres of worship were at Paphos and Amathus on Cyprus and on the island of Cythera, a Minoan colony, where in prehistoric times her cult probably originated. On the Greek mainland, Corinth was the chief centre of her worship. Her close association with Eros, the Graces (Charites), and the Horae (Seasons) emphasized her role as a promoter of fertility. She was

CENTAURS

Centaurs were a race of creatures, part horse and part man, dwelling in the mountains of Thessaly and Arcadia. Traditionally they were the off-spring of Ixion, king of the neighbouring Lapiths, and were best known for their fight (centauromachy) with the Lapiths, which resulted from their attempt to carry off the bride of Pirithous, son and successor of Ixion. They lost the battle and were driven from Mount Pelion. In later Greek times they were often represented drawing the chariot of the wine god Dionysus or bound and ridden by Eros, the god of love, in allusion to their drunken and amorous habits. Their general character was that of wild, lawless, and inhospitable beings, the slaves of their animal passions. (The Centaur Chiron was not typical in this respect.)

Centaurs may best be explained as the creation of a folktale in which wild inhabitants of the mountains and savage spirits of the forests were combined in half-human, half-animal form. In early art they were portrayed as human beings in front, with the body and hind legs of a horse attached to the back; later, they were men only as far as the waist. They fought using rough branches of trees as weapons.

honoured by the Roman poet Lucretius as Genetrix, the creative element in the world. Her epithets Urania (Heavenly Dweller) and Pandemos (Of All the People) were ironically taken by the philosopher Plato (in the *Symposium*) to refer to intellectual and common love; rather, the title Urania was honorific and applied to certain Asian deities, while Pandemos referred to her standing within the city-state. Among her symbols were the dove, pomegranate, swan, and myrtle.

Early Greek art represented Aphrodite either as the Oriental, nude-goddess type or as a standing or seated figure similar to all other goddesses. Aphrodite first attained individuality at the hands of the great 5th-century-BCE Greek sculptors. Perhaps the most famous of all statues of Aphrodite was carved by Praxiteles for the Cnidians; it later became the model for such Hellenistic masterpieces as the *Venus de Milo* (2nd century BCE).

APOLLO

A pollo was a deity of manifold function and meaning, after Zeus perhaps the most widely revered and influential of all the Greek gods. Though his original nature is obscure, from the time of Homer onward he was the god of divine distance, who sent or threatened from afar; the god who made men aware of their own guilt and purified them of it; who presided over religious law and the constitutions of cities; who communicated with mortals through prophets and oracles his knowledge of the future and the will of his father, Zeus. Even the gods feared him, and only his father and his mother, Leto, could easily endure his presence. Distance, death, terror, and awe were summed up in his symbolic bow; a gentler side of his nature, however, was shown in his other attribute, the lyre, which proclaimed the joy of communion with Olympus (the home of the gods) through music, poetry, and dance. In humbler circles he was also a god of crops and herds, primarily as a divine bulwark against wild animals and disease, as his epithet Alexikakos (Averter of Evil) indicates. His forename Phoebus means "bright" or "pure," and the view became current that he was connected with the sun.

Among Apollo's other epithets was Nomios (Herdsman), and he is said to have served King Admetus of Pherae in the lowly capacities of groom and herdsman as penance for slaying Zeus's armourers, the Cyclopes. He was also called Lyceius, presumably

The statuette known as the Apollo of Piombino, or the Piombino Boy, which depicts Apollo as a Kouros, or youth. Danita Delimont/Gallo Images/Getty Images

because he protected the flocks from wolves (*lykoi*); because herdsmen and shepherds beguiled the hours with music, scholars have argued that this was Apollo's original role.

Though Apollo was the most Hellenic of all gods, he derived mostly from a type of god that originated in Anatolia and spread to Egypt by way of Syria and Palestine. Traditionally, Apollo and his twin, Artemis, were born on the isle of Delos. From there Apollo went to Pytho (Delphi), where he slew Python, the dragon that guarded the area. He established his oracle by taking on the guise of a dolphin, leaping aboard a Cretan ship, and forcing the crew to serve him. Thus Pytho was renamed Delphi after the dolphin (*delphis*), and the Cretan cult of Apollo Delphinius superseded that previously established there by Earth (Gaea). During the Archaic period (8th to 6th century BCE), the fame of the Delphic oracle spread as far as Lydia in Anatolia and achieved pan-Hellenic status. The god's medium was the Pythia, a local woman over 50 years old, who, under his inspiration, delivered oracles in the main temple of Apollo. The oracles were subsequently interpreted and versified by priests. Other oracles of Apollo existed on the Greek mainland, Delos, and in Anatolia, but none rivalled Delphi in importance.

Of the Greek festivals in honour of Apollo, the most curious was the octennial Delphic Stepterion, in which a boy reenacted the slaying of the Python and was temporarily banished to the Vale of Tempe.

Although Apollo had many love affairs, they were mostly unfortunate: Daphne, in her efforts to escape him, was changed into a laurel, his sacred shrub; Coronis (mother of Asclepius) was shot by Apollo's twin, Artemis, when Coronis proved unfaithful; and

Cassandra (daughter of King Priam of Troy) rejected his advances and was punished by being made to utter true prophecies that no one believed.

In Italy Apollo was introduced at an early date and was primarily concerned, as in Greece, with healing and prophecy; he was highly revered by the emperor Augustus because the Battle of Actium (31 BCE) was fought near one of his temples. In art Apollo was represented as a beardless youth, either naked or robed, and often holding either a bow or a lyre.

ARES

A res was the god of war or, more properly, the spirit of battle. Unlike his Roman counterpart, Mars, he was never very popular, and his worship was not extensive in Greece. He represented the distasteful aspects of brutal warfare and slaughter. From at least the time of Homer, who established him as the son of the chief god, Zeus, and Hera, his consort, Ares was one of the Olympian deities; his fellow gods and even his parents, however, were not fond of him. Nonetheless, he was accompanied in battle by his sister Eris (Strife) and his sons (by Aphrodite) Phobos and Deimos (Panic and Rout). Also associated with him were two lesser war deities: Enyalius, who is virtually identical with Ares himself, and Enyo, a female counterpart.

Ares' worship was largely in the northern areas of Greece, and, although devoid of the social, moral, and theological associations usual with major deities, his cult had many interesting local features. At Sparta, in early times, at least, human sacrifices were made to him from among the prisoners of war. At Sparta also a nocturnal offering of dogs—an unusual sacrificial victim, which might indicate a chthonic (infernal) deity—was made to him as Enyalius. During his festival at Geronthrae in Laconia, no women were allowed in the sacred grove, but at Tegea he was honoured in a special women's sacrifice as Gynaikothoinas ("Entertainer of Women"). At Athens he had a temple at the foot of the Areopagus ("Ares' Hill").

The mythology surrounding the figure of Ares is not extensive. He was associated with Aphrodite from earliest times; in fact, Aphrodite was known locally (e.g., at Sparta) as a war goddess, apparently an early facet of her character. Occasionally, Aphrodite was Ares' legitimate wife, and by her he fathered Deimos, Phobos (who accompanied him into battle), Harmonia, and— as first told by Simonides in the 6th century BCE— Eros, god of love. By Aglauros, the daughter of Cecrops, he was the father of Alcippe. He was the sire of at least three of Heracles' adversaries: Cycnus, Lycaon, and Diomedes of Thrace. On vases, Ares is usually the typical armed warrior. The Parthenon frieze contains a group of Olympians, among whom Ares, in unwarlike garb, has been tentatively identified. He also appears on the great frieze of the altar at Pergamum.

Fifth-century-BCE ceramic container known as a pelike depicting Poseidon, Ares, and Hermes. DEA Picture Library/Getty Images

ARTEMIS

Artemis was the goddess of wild animals, the hunt, and vegetation, and of chastity and childbirth; she was identified by the Romans with Diana. Artemis was the daughter of Zeus and Leto and the twin sister of Apollo. Among the rural populace, Artemis was the favourite goddess. Her character and function varied greatly from place to place, but, apparently, behind all forms lay the goddess of wild nature, who danced, usually accompanied by nymphs, in mountains, forests, and marshes. Artemis embodied the sportsman's ideal, so besides killing game she also protected it, especially the young; this was the Homeric significance of the title Mistress of Animals.

The worship of Artemis probably flourished in Crete or on the Greek mainland in pre-Hellenic times. Many of Artemis's local cults, however, preserved traces of other deities, often with Greek names, suggesting that, upon adopting her, the Greeks identified Artemis with nature divinities of their own. The virginal sister of Apollo is very different from the many-breasted Artemis of Ephesus, for example.

Dances of maidens representing tree nymphs (dryads) were especially common in Artemis's worship as goddess of the tree cult, a role especially popular in the Peloponnese. Throughout the Peloponnese, bearing such epithets as Limnaea and Limnatis (Lady of the Lake), Artemis supervised waters and lush wild growth, attended by nymphs of wells and springs (naiads). In parts of the

A sculpture depicting the goddess Artemis of Ephesus. Peter Barritt/ SuperStock/Getty Images

peninsula her dances were wild and lascivious.

Outside the Peloponnese, Artemis's most familiar form was as Mistress of Animals. Poets and artists usually pictured her with the stag or hunting dog, but the cults showed considerable variety. For instance, the Tauropolia festival at Halae Araphenides in Attica honoured Artemis Tauropolos (Bull Goddess), who received a few drops of blood drawn by sword from a man's neck.

The frequent stories of the love affairs of Artemis's nymphs are supposed by some to have originally been told of the goddess herself. The poets after Homer, however, stressed Artemis's chastity and her delight in the hunt, dancing and music, shadowy groves, and the cities of just men. The wrath of Artemis was proverbial, for to it myth attributed wild nature's hostility to humans. Yet Greek sculpture avoided Artemis's unpitying anger as a motif; in fact, the goddess herself did not become popular as a subject in the great sculptural schools until the relatively gentle 4th-century-BCE spirit prevailed.

ASCLEPIUS

Asclepius was the Greco-Roman god of medicine, son of Apollo (god of healing, truth, and prophecy) and the mortal princess Coronis. The Centaur Chiron taught him the art of healing. At length Zeus (the king of the gods), afraid that Asclepius might render all men immortal, slew him with a thunderbolt. Apollo slew the Cyclopes who had made the thunderbolt and was then forced by Zeus to serve Admetus.

Homer, in the *Iliad*, mentions him only as a skillful physician and the father of two Greek doctors at Troy, Machaon and Podalirius; in later times, however, he was honoured as a hero and eventually worshipped as a god. The cult began in Thessaly but spread to many parts of Greece. Because it was supposed that Asclepius effected cures of the sick in dreams, the practice of sleeping in his temples in Epidaurus in South Greece became common. In 293 BCE his cult spread to Rome, where he was worshipped as Aesculapius.

Asclepius was frequently represented standing, dressed in a long cloak, with bare breast; his usual attribute was a staff with a serpent coiled around it. This staff is the only true symbol of medicine. A similar but unrelated emblem, the caduceus, with its winged staff and intertwined serpents, is frequently used as a medical emblem but is without medical relevance since it represents the magic wand of Hermes, or Mercury, the messenger of the gods and the patron of trade.

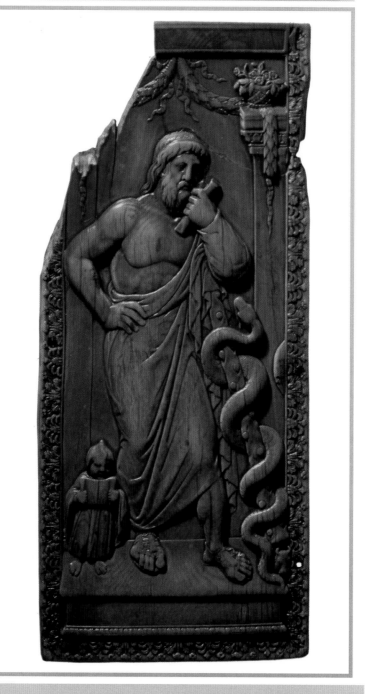

Asclepius, from an ivory diptych, 5th century CE; *in the Liverpool City Museum, England.* The Bridgeman Art Library/Art Resource, NY

ATHENA

Athena, also spelled Athene, was the city protectress, goddess of war, handicraft, and practical reason, identified by the Romans with Minerva. She was essentially urban and civilized, the antithesis in many respects of Artemis, goddess of the outdoors. Athena was probably a pre-Hellenic goddess and was later taken over by the Greeks. Yet the Greek economy, unlike that of the Minoans, was largely military, so that Athena, while retaining her earlier domestic functions, became a goddess of war.

She was the daughter of Zeus, produced without a mother, so that she emerged full-grown from his forehead. There was an alternative story that Zeus swallowed Metis, the goddess of counsel, while she was pregnant with Athena, so that Athena finally emerged from Zeus. Being the favourite child of Zeus, she had great power.

Athena's association with the acropolises of various Greek cities probably stemmed from the location of the kings' palaces there. She was thought to have had neither consort nor offspring. She may not have been described as a virgin originally, but virginity was attributed to her very early and was the basis for the interpretation of her epithets Pallas and Parthenos. As a war goddess Athena could not be dominated by other goddesses, such as Aphrodite, and as a palace goddess she could not be violated.

In Homer's *Iliad*, Athena, as a war goddess, inspired and fought alongside the Greek heroes; her aid was

Statue of Pallas Athena built by Danish architect Theophil Hansen at the Austrian Parliament building in Vienna, Austria. jorisvo/Shutterstock.com

synonymous with military prowess. Also in the *Iliad*, Zeus, the chief god, specifically assigned the sphere of war to Ares, the god of war, and Athena. Athena's moral and military superiority to Ares derived in part from the fact that she represented the intellectual and civilized side of war and the virtues of justice and skill, whereas Ares represented mere blood lust. Her superiority also derived in part from the vastly greater variety and importance of her functions and from the patriotism of Homer's predecessors, Ares being of foreign origin. In the *Iliad*, Athena was the divine form of the heroic, martial ideal: she personified excellence in close combat, victory, and glory. The qualities that led to victory were found on the aegis, or breastplate, that Athena wore when she went to war: fear, strife, defense, and assault. Athena appears in Homer's *Odyssey* as the tutelary deity of Odysseus, and myths from later sources portray her similarly as helper of Perseus and Heracles (Hercules). As the guardian of the welfare of kings, Athena became the goddess of good counsel, of prudent restraint and practical insight, as well as of war.

In post-Mycenaean times the city, especially its citadel, replaced the palace as Athena's domain. She was widely worshipped, but in modern times she is associated primarily with Athens, to which she gave her name. Her emergence there as city goddess, Athena Polias ("Athena, Guardian of the City"), accompanied the ancient city-state's transition from monarchy to democracy. She was associated with birds, particularly the owl, which became famous as the city's own symbol, and with the snake. Her birth and her contest with Poseidon, the sea god, for the suzerainty of the city were depicted on the pediments of the Parthenon, and the great festival of the Panathenaea, in July, was a celebration of her birthday. She was also worshipped in many other cities, notably in Sparta.

Athena became the goddess of crafts and skilled peacetime pursuits in general. She was particularly known as the patroness of spinning and weaving. That she ultimately became allegorized to personify wisdom and righteousness was a natural development of her patronage of skill.

Athena was customarily portrayed wearing body armour and a helmet and carrying a shield and a lance. Two Athenians, the sculptor Phidias and the playwright Aeschylus, contributed significantly to the cultural dissemination of Athena's image. She inspired three of Phidias's sculptural masterpieces, including the massive chryselephantine (gold and ivory) statue of Athena Parthenos housed in the Parthenon; and in Aeschylus's dramatic tragedy *Eumenides* she founded the Areopagus (Athens' aristocratic council), and, by breaking a deadlock of the judges in favour of Orestes, the defendant, she set the precedent that a tied vote signified acquittal.

ATLAS

Atlas was the son of the Titan Iapetus and the Oceanid Clymene (or Asia) and brother of Prometheus (creator of humankind). In Homer's *Odyssey*, Book I, Atlas seems to have been a marine creature who supported the pillars that held heaven and Earth apart. These were thought to rest in the sea immediately beyond the most western horizon, but later the name of Atlas was transferred to a range of mountains in northwestern Africa. Atlas was subsequently represented as the king of that district, turned into a rocky mountain by the hero Perseus, who, to punish Atlas for his inhospitality, showed him the Gorgon's head, the sight of which turned men to stone. According to Hesiod's *Theogony*, Atlas was one of the Titans who took part in their war against Zeus, for which as a punishment he was condemned to hold aloft the heavens. In many works of art he was represented as carrying the heavens (in Classical art from the 6th century BCE) or the celestial globe (in Hellenistic and Roman art).

THE MUSES

In Greco-Roman religion and mythology, the Muses were any of a group of sister goddesses of obscure but ancient origin, the chief centre of whose cult was Mount Helicon in Boeotia, Greece. They were born in Pieria, at the foot of Mount Olympus. Very little is known of their cult, but they had a festival every four years at Thespiae, near Helicon, and a contest (Museia), presumably—or at least at first—in singing and playing. They probably were originally the patron goddesses of poets (who in early times were also musicians, providing their own accompaniments), although later their range was extended to include all liberal arts and sciences—hence, their connection with such institutions as the Museum (*Mouseion*, seat of the Muses) at Alexandria, Egypt. There were nine Muses as early as Homer's *Odyssey*, and Homer invokes either a Muse or the Muses collectively from time to time. Probably, to begin with, the Muses were one of those vague collections of deities, undifferentiated within the group, which are characteristic of certain, probably early, strata of Greek religion.

Differentiation is a matter rather of mythological systematization than of cult and began with the 8th-century-BCE poet Hesiod, who mentioned the names of Clio, Euterpe, Thalia, Melpomene, Terpsichore, Erato, Polymnia (Polyhymnia), Urania, and Calliope, who was their chief. Their father was Zeus, and their mother was Mnemosyne ("Memory"). Although Hesiod's list became canonical in later times, it was not the only one; at both Delphi and Sicyon there were but three Muses, one of whom in the latter place bore the fanciful name Polymatheia ("Much Learning"). All the Hesiodic names are significant; thus Clio is approximately the "Proclaimer," Euterpe the "Well Pleasing," Thalia the "Blooming," or "Luxuriant," Melpomene the "Songstress," Erato the "Lovely," Polymnia "She of the Many Hymns," Urania the "Heavenly," and Calliope "She of the Beautiful Voice." Because dancing was a regular accompaniment of song, it is not remarkable that Hesiod called one of his nine "Delighting in the Dance," Terpsichore.

The Muses are often spoken of as unmarried, but they are repeatedly referred to as the mothers of famous sons, such as Orpheus, Rhesus, Eumolpus, and others connected somehow either with poetry and song or with Thrace and its neighbourhood, or both. In other words, all their myths are secondary, attached for one reason or another to the original vague and nameless group. Hence there is no consistency in these minor tales—Terpsichore, for example, is named as the mother of several different men by various authors and Orpheus generally is called the son of Calliope but occasionally of Polymnia.

Statues of the Muses were a popular decoration in long galleries and similar places; naturally, sculptors did not make them all alike but gave each a different attribute, such as a lyre or scroll. This may have contributed to the fanciful distribution of individual Muses among the different arts and sciences, especially in Roman times. The lists that have come down are all late and disagree with one another. A common but by no means definitive list is the following:

- Calliope: Muse of heroic or epic poetry (often holding a writing tablet)
- Clio: Muse of history (often holding a scroll)
- Erato: Muse of lyric and love poetry (often playing a lyre)
- Euterpe: Muse of music or flutes (often playing flutes)
- Melpomene: Muse of tragedy (often holding a tragic mask)
- Polymnia: Muse of sacred poetry or of the mimic art (often shown with a pensive look)
- Terpsichore: Muse of dancing and choral song (often shown dancing and holding a lyre)
- Thalia: Muse of comedy (often holding a comic mask)
- Urania: Muse of astronomy (often holding a globe)

CALLIOPE

Calliope, also spelled Kalliope, was, according to Hesiod's *Theogony*, foremost of the nine Muses; she was later called the patron of epic poetry. At the behest of Zeus, the king of the gods, she judged the dispute between the goddesses Aphrodite and Persephone over Adonis. In most accounts she and King Oeagrus of Thrace were the parents of Orpheus, the lyre-playing hero. She was also loved by the god Apollo, by whom she had two sons, Hymen and Ialemus. Other versions present her as the mother of Rhesus, king of Thrace and a victim of the Trojan War, or as the mother of Linus the musician, who was the inventor of melody and rhythm. Her image appears on the François Vase, made by the potter Ergotimos about 570 BCE.

CLIO

Clio was one of the nine Muses, patron of history. Traditionally Clio, after reprimanding the goddess Aphrodite for her passionate love for Adonis, was punished by Aphrodite, who made her fall in love with Pierus, king of Macedonia. From that union, in some accounts, was born Hyacinthus, a young man of great beauty who was later killed by his lover, the god Apollo. From his blood sprang a flower (the hyacinth). In art Clio was frequently represented with the heroic trumpet and the clepsydra (water clock).

CRONUS

Cronus, also spelled Cronos or Kronos, was a male deity who was worshipped by the pre-Hellenic population of Greece but probably was not widely worshipped by the Greeks themselves; he was later identified with the Roman god Saturn. Cronus's functions were connected with agriculture; in Attica his festival, the Kronia, celebrated the harvest and resembled the Saturnalia. In art he was depicted as an old man holding an implement, probably originally a sickle but interpreted as a harpe, or curved sword.

In Greek mythology Cronus was the son of Uranus (Heaven) and Gaea (Earth), being the youngest of the 12 Titans. On the advice of his mother he castrated his father with a harpe, thus separating Heaven from Earth. He now became the king of the Titans and took for his consort his sister Rhea; she bore by him Hestia, Demeter, Hera, Hades, and Poseidon, all of whom he swallowed because his own parents had warned that he would be overthrown by his own child. When Zeus was born, however, Rhea hid him in Crete and tricked Cronus into swallowing a stone instead. Zeus grew up, forced Cronus to disgorge his brothers and sisters, waged war on Cronus, and was victorious. After his defeat by Zeus, Cronus became, according to different versions of his story, either a prisoner in Tartarus or king in Elysium. According to one tradition, the period of Cronus's rule was a golden age for mortals.

Oil-on-canvas painting by Giacinto Brandi of the god Cronus. Universal Images Group/Getty Images

CYCLOPS

The Cyclops was any of several one-eyed giants to whom were ascribed a variety of histories and deeds. In Homer the Cyclopes were cannibals, living a rude pastoral life in a distant land (traditionally Sicily), and the *Odyssey* contains a well-known episode in which Odysseus escapes death by blinding the Cyclops Polyphemus. In Hesiod the Cyclopes were three sons of Uranus and Gaea—Arges, Brontes, and Steropes (Bright, Thunderer, Lightener)—who forged the thunderbolts of Zeus. Later authors made them the workmen of Hephaestus and said that Apollo killed them for making the thunderbolt that slew his son Asclepius.

The walls of several ancient cities (e.g., Tiryns) of Mycenaean architecture were sometimes said to have been built by Cyclopes. Hence in modern archaeology the term *cyclopean* is applied to walling of which the stones are not squared.

DEMETER

Demeter was the daughter of the deities Cronus and Rhea, sister and consort of Zeus (the king of the gods), and goddess of agriculture. Her name indicates that she is a mother.

Demeter is rarely mentioned by Homer, nor is she included among the Olympian gods, but the roots of her legend are probably ancient. The legend centred on the story of her daughter Persephone, who was carried off by Hades, the god of the underworld. Demeter went in search of Persephone and, during her journey, revealed her secret rites to the people of Eleusis, who had hospitably received her. Her distress at her daughter's disappearance was said to have diverted her attention from the harvest and caused a famine. In addition to Zeus, Demeter had a lover, Iasion (a Cretan), to whom she bore Plutus (Wealth; i.e., abundant produce of the soil).

Demeter appeared most commonly as a grain goddess. The name Ioulo (from *ioulos*, "grain sheaf") has been regarded as identifying her with the sheaf and as proving that the cult of Demeter originated in the worship of the grain mother. The influence of Demeter, however, was not limited to grain but extended to vegetation generally and to all the fruits of the earth, except the bean (the latter being the province of the hero Cyamites). In that wider sense Demeter was akin to Gaea (Earth), with whom she had several epithets in common, and was sometimes identified with the Great Mother of the Gods (Cybele, also identified with Rhea).

Sixth-century-BCE statue of the goddess Demeter. DEA/G. Dagli Orti/De Agostini/Getty Images

Another important aspect of Demeter was that of a divinity of the underworld; she was worshipped as such at Sparta, and especially at the festival of Chthonia at Hermione in Argolis, where a cow was sacrificed by four old women. The epithets Erinys ("Avenger") and Melaina ("the Black One") as applied to Demeter were localized in Arcadia and stress the darker side of her character.

Demeter also appeared as a goddess of health, birth, and marriage. A certain number of political and ethnic titles were assigned to her, the most important being Amphiktyonis, as patron goddess of the Amphictyonic League, subsequently well known in connection with the temple at Delphi.

Among the agrarian festivals held in honour of Demeter were the following:

1. Haloa, apparently derived from *halos* ("threshing floor"), begun at Athens and finished at Eleusis, where there was a threshing floor of Triptolemus, her first priest and inventor of agriculture; it was held in the month Poseideon (December).

2. Chloia, the festival of the grain beginning to sprout, held at Eleusis in the early spring (Anthesterion) in honour of Demeter Chloë ("the Green"), the goddess of growing vegetation. This festival is to be distinguished from the later sacrifice of a ram to the same goddess on the sixth of the month Thargelion, probably intended as an act of propitiation.

3. Proerosia, at which prayers were offered for an abundant harvest, before the land was plowed for sowing. It was also called Proarktouria, an indication that it was held before the rising of Arcturus. The festival took place, probably sometime in September, at Eleusis.

4. Thalysia, a thanksgiving festival held in autumn after the harvest in the island of Cos.

5. The Thesmophoria, a women's festival meant to improve the fruitfulness of the seed grain.

6. The Skirophoria held in midsummer, a companion festival.

Her attributes were connected chiefly with her character as goddess of agriculture and vegetation—ears of grain, the mystic basket filled with flowers, grain, and fruit of all kinds. The pig was her favourite animal, and as a chthonian (underworld) deity she was accompanied by a snake. In Greek art Demeter resembled Hera, but she was more matronly and of milder expression; her form was broader and fuller. She was sometimes riding in a chariot drawn by horses or dragons, sometimes walking, or sometimes seated upon a throne, alone or with her daughter. The Romans identified Demeter with Ceres.

DIONYSUS

Dionysus, also spelled Dionysos, also called Bacchus or (in Rome) Liber, was, in Greco-Roman religion, a nature god of fruitfulness and vegetation, especially known as a god of wine and ecstasy. The occurrence of his name on a Linear B tablet (13th century BCE) shows that he was already worshipped in the Mycenaean period, although it is not known where his cult originated. In all the legends of his cult, he is depicted as having foreign origins.

Dionysus was the son of Zeus and Semele, a daughter of Cadmus (king of Thebes). Out of jealousy, Hera, the wife of Zeus, persuaded the pregnant Semele to prove her lover's divinity by requesting that he appear in his real person. Zeus complied, but his power was too great for the mortal Semele, who was blasted with thunderbolts. However, Zeus saved his son by sewing him up in his thigh and keeping him there until he reached maturity, so that he was twice born. Dionysus was then conveyed by the god Hermes to be brought up by the bacchantes (maenads, or *thyiads*) of Nysa, a purely imaginary spot.

As Dionysus apparently represented the sap, juice, or lifeblood element in nature, lavish festal *orgia* (rites) in his honour were widely instituted. These Dionysia (Bacchanalia) quickly won converts among women. Men, however, met them with hostility. In Thrace Dionysus was opposed by Lycurgus, who ended up blind and mad.

In Thebes Dionysus was opposed by Pentheus, his cousin, who was torn to pieces by the bacchantes when he attempted to spy on their activities. The Athenians

A marble statue of the god Dionysus. Peter Barritt/SuperStock

were punished with impotence for dishonouring the god's cult. Their husbands' resistance notwithstanding, women took to the hills, wearing fawn skins and crowns of ivy and shouting the ritual cry, "Euoi!" Forming *thyai* (holy bands) and waving *thyrsoi* (singular: *thyrsus*; fennel wands bound with grapevine and tipped with ivy), they danced by torchlight to the rhythm of the *aulos* (double pipe) and the *tympanon* (handheld drum). While they were under the god's inspiration, the bacchantes were believed to possess occult powers and the ability to charm snakes and suckle animals, as well as preternatural strength that enabled them to tear living victims to pieces before indulging in a ritual feast (*omophagia*). The bacchantes hailed the god by his titles of Bromios ("Thunderer"), Taurokeros ("Bull-Horned"), or Tauroprosopos ("Bull-Faced"), in the belief that he incarnated the sacrificial beast.

In Orphic legend (i.e., based on the stories of Orpheus) Dionysus—under the name Zagreus—was the son of

ECHO

In Greek mythology, Echo is a mountain nymph, or Oread. Ovid's *Metamorphoses*, Book III, relates that Echo offended the goddess Hera by keeping her in conversation, thus preventing her from spying on one of Zeus's amours. To punish Echo, Hera deprived her of speech, except for the ability to repeat the last words of another. Echo's hopeless love for Narcissus, who fell in love with his own image, made her fade away until all that was left of her was her voice.

According to the Greek writer Longus, Echo rejected the advances of the god Pan; he thereupon drove the shepherds mad, and they tore her to pieces. Gaea (Earth) buried her limbs but allowed her to retain the power of song.

Zeus by his daughter Persephone. At the direction of Hera, the infant Zagreus/Dionysus was torn to pieces, cooked, and eaten by the evil Titans. But his heart was saved by Athena, and he (now Dionysus) was resurrected by Zeus through Semele. Zeus struck the Titans with lightning, and they were consumed by fire. From their ashes came the first men, who thus possessed both the evil nature of the Titans and the divine nature of the gods.

Dionysus had the power to inspire and to create ecstasy, and his cult had special importance for art and literature. Performances of tragedy and comedy in Athens were part of two festivals of Dionysus, the Lenaea and the Great (or City) Dionysia. He was also honoured in lyric poems called dithyrambs. In Roman literature his nature is often misunderstood, and he is simplistically portrayed as the jolly Bacchus who is invoked at drinking parties. In 186 BCE the celebration of Bacchanalia was prohibited in Italy.

The followers of Dionysus included spirits of fertility, such as the satyrs and sileni, and in his rituals the phallus was prominent. He often took on a bestial shape and was associated with various animals. His personal attributes were an ivy wreath, the thyrsus, and the *kantharos*, a large two-handled goblet. In early art he was represented as a bearded man, but later he was portrayed as youthful and effeminate. Bacchic revels were a favourite subject of vase painters.

EOS

Eos was the personification of the dawn. According to the Greek poet Hesiod's *Theogony*, she was the daughter of the Titan Hyperion and the Titaness Theia and sister of Helios, the sun god, and Selene, the moon goddess. By the Titan Astraeus she was the mother of the winds Zephyrus, Notus, and Boreas, and of Hesperus (the Evening Star) and the other stars; by Tithonus of Assyria she was the mother of Memnon, king of the Ethiopians,

*A 5th-century-*BCE *kylix, or drinking cup, known as the Memnon pietà, depicting Eos raising the body of her son Memnon.* DEA Picture Library/ Getty Images

who was slain by Achilles at Troy. She bears in Homer's works the epithet Rosy-Fingered.

Eos was also represented as the lover of the hunter Orion and of the youthful hunter Cephalus, by whom she was the mother of Phaethon (not the same as the son of Helios). Her most famous lover was the Trojan Tithonus, for whom she gained from Zeus the gift of immortality but forgot to ask for eternal youth. As a result, Tithonus grew ever older and weaker, but he could not die. In works of art Eos is represented as a young woman, usually winged, either walking fast with a youth in her arms or rising from the sea in a chariot drawn by winged horses; sometimes, as the goddess who dispenses the dews of the morning, she has a pitcher in each hand.

In Latin writings the name Aurora was used (e.g., by Virgil) for the east.

EROS

Eros was the god of love. In the *Theogony* of Hesiod, Eros was a primeval god, son of Chaos, the original primeval emptiness of the universe, but later tradition made him the son of Aphrodite, goddess of sexual love and beauty, by either Zeus (the king of the gods), Ares (god of war and of battle), or Hermes (divine messenger of the gods). Eros was a god not simply of passion but also of fertility. His brother was Anteros, the god of mutual love, who was sometimes described as his opponent. The chief associates of Eros were Pothos and Himeros (Longing and Desire). Later writers assumed the existence of a number of Erotes (like the several versions of the Roman Amor). In

Marble statue of the god Eros. Peter Barritt/SuperStock

Alexandrian poetry he degenerated into a mischievous child. In Archaic art he was represented as a beautiful winged youth but tended to be made younger and younger until, by the Hellenistic period, he was an infant. His chief cult centre was at Thespiae in Boeotia, where the Erotidia were celebrated. He also shared a sanctuary with Aphrodite on the north wall of the Acropolis at Athens.

EUTERPE

Euterpe was one of the nine Muses, patron of tragedy or flute playing. In some accounts she was the mother of Rhesus, the king of Thrace, killed in the Trojan War, whose father was sometimes identified as Strymon, the river god of Thrace.

FURIES

The Furies, in Greco-Roman mythology, were goddesses of vengeance. They were probably personified curses, but possibly they were originally conceived of as ghosts of the murdered. According to the Greek poet Hesiod they were the daughters of Gaea (Earth) and sprang from the blood of her mutilated spouse Uranus; in the plays of Aeschylus they were the daughters of Nyx; in those of Sophocles, they were the daughters of Darkness and of Gaea. Euripides was the first to speak of them as three in number. Later writers named them Allecto ("Unceasing in Anger"), Tisiphone ("Avenger of Murder"), and Megaera ("Jealous"). They lived in the underworld and ascended to Earth to pursue the wicked. Being deities of the underworld, they were often identified with spirits of the fertility of the Earth. Because the Greeks feared to utter the dreaded name Erinyes, the goddesses were often addressed by the euphemistic names Eumenides ("Kind Ones") or Semnai Theai ("Venerable Goddesses").

GAEA

G aea, also called Ge, was the personification of the
Earth as a goddess. Mother and wife of Uranus

(Heaven), from whom the Titan Cronus, her last-born child by him, separated her, she was also mother of the other Titans, the Gigantes, the Erinyes, and the Cyclopes. Gaea may have been originally a mother goddess worshipped in Greece before the Hellenes introduced the cult of Zeus. Less widely worshipped in historic times, Gaea was described as the giver of dreams and the nourisher of plants and young children.

Gaea is often shown as being present at the birth of Zeus, but in some legends she is his enemy because she is the mother of the giants and of the 100-headed monster Typhon.

Fresco depicting Poseidon, god of the sea, with Gaea. Stefan Auth/ imagebroker.net/SuperStock

HADES

ades was the son of the Titans Cronus and Rhea, and brother of the deities Zeus, Poseidon, Demeter, Hera, and Hestia. After Cronus was killed, the kingdom of the underworld fell by lot to Hades. There he ruled with his queen, Persephone, over the infernal powers and over the dead, in what was often called "the House of Hades," or simply Hades. He was aided by the dog Cerberus. Though Hades supervised the trial and punishment of the wicked after death, he was not normally one of the judges in the underworld; nor did he personally torture the guilty, a task assigned to the Furies (Erinyes). Hades was depicted as stern and pitiless, unmoved (like death itself) by prayer or sacrifice. Forbidding and aloof, he never quite emerges as a distinct personality from the shadowy darkness of his realm, not even in the myth of his abduction of Persephone.

He was usually worshipped under a euphemistic epithet such as Clymenus ("the Illustrious") or Eubuleus ("the Giver of Good Counsel"). He was often called Zeus, with the addition of a special title (e.g., chthonios). His title Pluto, or Pluton ("the Wealthy One," or "the Giver of Wealth"), may have originated through Hades' partial amalgamation with a god of the Earth's fertility or because he gathered all living things into his treasury at death.

The word *Hades* is used in the Greek Old Testament to translate the Hebrew word *sheol*, denoting a dark region of the dead. Tartarus, originally an abyss far below Hades and the place of punishment in the lower world, later lost its distinctness and became almost a synonym for Hades.

First-century-BCE statue of the god Hades. DEA/G. Dagli Orti/De Agostini/Getty Images

TEMPLES AND SHRINES

In the earliest times deities were worshipped in awesome places such as groves, caves, or mountaintops. Mycenaean deities shared the king's palace. Fundamental was the precinct (*temenos*) allotted to the deity, containing the altar, temple (if any), and other sacral or natural features, such as the sacred olive in the *temenos* of Pandrosos on the Athenian Acropolis. *Naoi* (temples—literally "dwellings"—that housed the god's image) were already known in Homeric times and, like models discovered at Perachora, were wooden and of simple design. Poros and marble replaced wood by the end of the 7th century BCE, when temples became large and were constructed with rows of columns on all sides. The image, crude and wooden at first, was placed in the central chamber (*cella*), which was open at the eastern end. No ritual was associated with the image itself, though it was sometimes paraded. Hero shrines were far less elaborate and had pits for offerings. Miniature shrines also were known.

Most oracular shrines included a subterranean chamber, but no trace of such has been found at Delphi, though the Pythia was always said to "descend." At the oracle of Trophonius, discovered in 1967 at Levádhia, incubation (ritual sleep to induce a dream) was practiced in a hole. The most famous centre of incubation was that of Asclepius at Epidaurus. His temple was furnished with a hall where the sick were advised by the demigod in dreams. Divination was also widely practiced in Greece. Augurs interpreted the flight of birds, while dreams and even sneezes were regarded as ominous. Seers also divined from the shape of altar smoke and the conformation of sacrificial animals' entrails.

HEBE

Hebe, meaning "young maturity," or "bloom of youth," was the daughter of Zeus, the chief god, and his wife Hera.

Statue of goddess Hebe in Ballarat, Victoria, Australia. K.A. Willis/ Shutterstock.com

In Homer this princess was a divine domestic, appearing most often as cupbearer to the gods. As the goddess of youth, she was generally worshipped along with her mother, of whom she may have been regarded as an emanation or specialized form. She was also associated with the hero-god Heracles, whose bride she became when he was received into heaven. Her major centres of worship were Phlious and Sicyon, where she was called Ganymeda and Dia. Hebe was sometimes identified with the Roman deity Juventas.

HEPHAESTUS

Hephaestus (also Hephaistos) was the god of fire. Originally a deity of Asia Minor and the adjoining islands (in particular Lemnos), he had an important place of worship at the Lycian Olympus. Born lame, Hephaestus was cast from heaven in disgust by his mother, Hera, and again by his father, Zeus, after a family quarrel; he was brought back by Dionysus. His ill-matched consort was Aphrodite, or else Charis, the personification of Grace.

As god of fire, Hephaestus became the divine smith and patron of craftsmen; the natural volcanic or gaseous fires already connected with him were often considered to be his workshops. His cult reached Athens not later than about 600 BCE (although it scarcely touched Greece proper) and arrived in Campania not long afterward. In art Hephaestus was generally represented as a middle-aged, bearded man, although occasionally a younger, beardless type is found. He usually wore a short, sleeveless tunic and a round, close-fitting cap on his unkempt hair. His Roman counterpart was Vulcan.

HERA

era was a daughter of the Titans Cronus and Rhea, sister-wife of Zeus, and queen of the Olympian gods. The Romans identified her with their own Juno. Hera was worshipped throughout the Greek world and played an important part in Greek literature, appearing most frequently as the jealous and rancorous wife of Zeus and pursuing with vindictive hatred the heroines who were beloved by him. From early times Hera was believed to be the sole lawful wife of Zeus; she soon superseded Dione, who shared with him his ancient oracle at Dodona in Epirus.

In general, Hera was worshipped in two main capacities: (1) as consort of Zeus and queen of heaven and (2) as goddess of marriage and of the life of women. The second sphere naturally made her the protectress of women in childbirth, and she bore the title of Eileithyia, the birth goddess, at Argos and Athens. At

Copy of a Roman bust of Roman goddess Juno (Hera in Greek mythology) located in Rome, Italy. Album/Oronoz/Album/SuperStock

Argos and Samos, however, Hera was even more than queen of heaven and marriage goddess. She was patron of those cities, which gave her a position corresponding to that of Athena at Athens. Although her Argive ritual was markedly agricultural, she also had a celebration there called the Shield, and there was an armed procession in her honour at Samos. This conception resulted from the breadth of functions attributed to the patron deity of a Greek state: a city goddess must be chief in peace and war alike. The animal especially sacred to Hera was the cow. Her sacred bird was first the cuckoo, later the peacock. She was represented as a majestic and severe, though youthful, matron.

HERACLES

Heracles was one of the most famous Greco-Roman legendary heroes. Traditionally, Heracles was the son of Zeus and Alcmene, granddaughter of Perseus. Zeus swore that the next son born of the Perseid house should become ruler of Greece, but by a trick of Zeus's jealous wife, Hera, another child, the sickly Eurystheus, was born first and became king; when Heracles grew up, he had to serve him and also suffer the vengeful persecution of Hera. His first exploit, in fact, was the strangling of two serpents that she had sent to kill him in his cradle.

Later, Heracles waged a victorious war against the kingdom of Orchomenus in Boeotia and married Megara, daughter of Creon, king of Thebes. But he killed her and their children in a fit of madness sent by Hera and, consequently, was obliged to become the servant of Eurystheus. It was Eurystheus who imposed upon Heracles the famous Labours, later arranged in a cycle of 12, usually as follows: (1) the slaying of the Nemean lion, whose skin he thereafter wore; (2) the slaying of the nine-headed Hydra of Lerna; (3) the capture of the elusive hind (or stag) of Arcadia; (4) the capture of the wild boar of Mt. Erymanthus; (5) the cleansing, in a single day, of the cattle stables of King Augeas of Elis; (6) the shooting of the monstrous man-eating birds of the Stymphalian marshes; (7) the capture of the mad bull that terrorized the island of Crete; (8) the capture of the man-eating mares of King Diomedes of the Bistones; (9) the taking of the girdle of Hippolyte, queen of the Amazons; (10)

the seizing of the cattle of the three-bodied giant Geryon, who ruled the island Erytheia (meaning Red) in the far west; (11) the bringing back of the golden apples kept at the world's end by the Hesperides; and (12) the fetching up from the lower world of the triple-headed dog Cerberus, guardian of its gates.

Having completed the Labours, Heracles undertook further enterprises, including warlike campaigns. He

Detail from a Greek water jug found at the Etruscan city Vulci, c. 490 BCE, of Heracles struggling with the god Nerus. Courtesy of the trustees of the British Museum

also successfully fought the river god Achelous for the hand of Deianeira. As he was taking her home, the Centaur Nessus tried to violate her, and Heracles shot him with one of his poisoned arrows. The Centaur, dying, told Deianeira to preserve the blood from his wound, for if Heracles wore a garment rubbed with it he would love none but her forever. Several years later Heracles fell in love with Iole, daughter of Eurytus, king of Oechalia. Deianeira, realizing that Iole was a dangerous rival, sent Heracles a garment smeared with the blood of Nessus. The blood proved to be a powerful poison, and Heracles died. His body was placed on a pyre on Mt. Oeta (modern Greek Oiti), his mortal part was consumed, and his divine part ascended to heaven. There he was reconciled to Hera and married Hebe.

In art and literature Heracles was represented as an enormously strong man of moderate height; a huge eater and drinker, very amorous, generally kindly but with occasional outbursts of brutal rage. His characteristic weapon was the bow but frequently also the club.

In Italy he was worshipped as a god of merchants and traders, although others also prayed to him for his characteristic gifts of good luck or rescue from danger.

HERMES

Greek god, son of Zeus and the Pleiad Maia, Hermes was often identified with the Roman Mercury and with Casmilus or Cadmilus, one of the Cabeiri. His name is probably derived from *herma*, the Greek word for a heap of stones, such as was used in the country to indicate boundaries or as a landmark. The earliest centre of his cult was probably Arcadia, where Mt. Cyllene was reputed to be his birthplace. There he was especially worshipped as the god of fertility, and his images were ithyphallic.

Both in literature and cult Hermes was constantly associated with the protection of cattle and sheep, and he was often closely connected with deities of vegetation, especially Pan and the nymphs. In the *Odyssey*, however, he appears mainly as the messenger of the gods and the conductor of the dead to Hades. Hermes was also a dream god, and the Greeks offered to him the last libation before sleep. As a messenger, he may also have become the god of roads and doorways, and he was the protector of travellers. Treasure casually found was his gift, and any stroke of good luck was attributed to him; this conception and his function as a deity of gain, honest or dishonest, are natural derivatives of his character as a god of fertility. In many respects he was Apollo's counterpart; like him, Hermes was a patron of music and was credited with the invention of the kithara and sometimes of music itself. He was also god of eloquence and presided over some kinds of popular divination.

Fifth-century-BCE marble bust of the god Hermes. DEA/G. Dagli Orti/De Agostini/Getty Images

The sacred number of Hermes was four, and the fourth day of the month was his birthday. In Archaic art, apart from the stylized herms, he was portrayed as a full-grown and bearded man, clothed in a long tunic and often wearing a cap and winged boots. Sometimes he was represented in his pastoral character, bearing a sheep on his shoulders; at other times he appeared as the messenger of the gods with the *kerykeion*, or herald's staff, which was his most frequent attribute. From the latter part of the 5th century BCE he was portrayed as a nude and beardless youth, a young athlete.

HESTIA

Hestia was the goddess of the hearth, daughter of Cronus and Rhea, and one of the 12 Olympian deities. When the gods Apollo and Poseidon became suitors for her hand she swore to remain a maiden forever, whereupon Zeus, the king of the gods, bestowed upon her the honour of presiding over all sacrifices.

She was worshipped chiefly as goddess of the family hearth; but, as the city union was only the family union on a large scale, she had also, at least in some states, a public cult at the civic hearth in the *prytaneion*, or town hall. Hestia was closely connected with Zeus, god of the family in its external relation of hospitality and its internal unity. She was also associated with Hermes, the two representing domestic life on the one hand, and business and outdoor life on the other. In later philosophy Hestia became the hearth goddess of the universe.

Vase with detail of the goddess Hestia. DEA/G. Dagli Orti/De Agostini/Getty Images

HYGIEIA

Hygieia was the goddess of health. The oldest traces of her cult are at Titane, west of Corinth, where she was worshipped together with Asclepius, the god of medicine. At first no special relationship existed between her and Asclepius, but gradually she came to be regarded as his daughter; later literature, however, makes her his wife. The cult of Hygieia spread concurrently with his and was introduced at Rome from Epidaurus in 293 BCE, when she was gradually identified with Salus. In later times, Hygieia and Asclepius became protecting deities. Hygieia's animal was a serpent, sometimes shown drinking from a saucer held in her hand.

Marble statue of the goddess Hygieia. DEA Picture Library/Getty Images

HYPNOS

Hypnos was the Greco-Roman god of sleep. Hypnos was the son of Nyx (Night) and the twin brother of Thanatos (Death). In Greek myth he is variously described as living in the underworld or on the island of Lemnos (according to Homer) or (according to Book XI of Ovid's *Metamorphoses*) in a dark, musty cave in the land of the Cimmerians, through which flowed the waters of Lethe, the river of forgetfulness and oblivion. Hypnos lay on his soft couch, surrounded by his many sons, who were the bringers of dreams. Chief among them were Morpheus, who brought dreams of men; Icelus, who brought dreams of animals; and Phantasus, who brought dreams of inanimate things.

In Book XIV of Homer's *Iliad*, Hypnos is enlisted by Hera to lull Zeus to sleep so that she can aid the Greeks in their war against Troy. As a reward for his services, Hypnos is given Pasithea, one of the Graces, to wed. In Book XVI of the *Iliad*, Hypnos and Thanatos carry the body of Sarpedon home to Lycia after he is slain by Patroclus, a scene depicted in the 6th century BCE by the Greek artist Euphronius and others.

MELPOMENE

Melpomene was one of the nine Muses, patron of tragedy and lyre playing. In Greek art her attributes were the tragic mask and the club of Heracles. According to some traditions, the half-bird, half-woman Sirens were born from the union of Melpomene with the river god Achelous.

MNEMOSYNE

Mnemosyne was the goddess of memory. A Titaness, she was the daughter of Uranus (Heaven) and Gaea (Earth), and, according to Hesiod, the mother (by Zeus) of the nine Muses. She gave birth to the Muses after Zeus went to Pieria and stayed with her nine consecutive nights.

MORPHEUS

Morpheus was one of the sons of Hypnos (Somnus), the god of sleep. Morpheus sends human shapes (Greek *morphai*) of all kinds to the dreamer, while his brothers Phobetor (or Icelus) and Phantasus send the forms of animals and inanimate things, respectively.

NEMESIS

Nemesis was two divine conceptions, the first an Attic goddess, the daughter of Nyx (Night), and the second an abstraction of indignant disapproval, later personified. Nemesis the goddess (perhaps of fertility) was worshipped at Rhamnus in Attica and was very similar to Artemis (a goddess of wild animals, vegetation, childbirth, and the hunt). In the post-Homeric epic *Cypria*, reported in Apollodorus's *Library*, Book III, Nemesis turned herself into a goose to escape the clutches of Zeus; he eventually turned himself into a swan and caught her. Nemesis then laid an egg that was brought to Leda and from which Helen was hatched.

That Nemesis the abstraction was worshipped, at least in later times, is beyond doubt. She signified particularly the disapproval of the gods at human presumption, and her first altar was said to have been erected in Boeotia by Adrastus, leader of the Seven Against Thebes. In Rome, especially, her cult was very popular, particularly among soldiers, by whom she was worshipped as patroness of the drill ground (Nemesis Campestris).

NIKE

Nike was the goddess of victory, daughter of the giant Pallas and of the infernal River Styx. Nike probably did not originally have a separate cult at

Marble statue of the goddess Nike. Henner Damke/Shutterstock.com

Athens. As an attribute of both Athena, the goddess of wisdom, and the chief god, Zeus, Nike was represented in art as a small figure carried in the hand by those divinities. Athena Nike was always wingless; Nike alone was winged. She also appears carrying a palm branch, wreath, or Hermes staff as the messenger of victory. Nike is also portrayed erecting a trophy, or, frequently, hovering with outspread wings over the victor in a competition; for her functions referred to success not only in war but in all other undertakings. Indeed, Nike gradually came to be recognized as a sort of mediator of success between gods and men.

At Rome, where Nike was called Victoria, she was worshipped from the earliest times. She came to be regarded as the protecting goddess of the Senate, and her statue in the Curia Julia (originally set up by Augustus in memory of the Battle of Actium) was the cause of the final combat between Christianity and paganism toward the end of the 4th century.

Among artistic representations of Nike are the sculpture by Paeonius (c. 424 BCE) and the Nike of Samothrace. The latter, discovered on Samothrace in 1863 and now in the Louvre Museum, Paris, was probably erected by Rhodians about 203 BC to commemorate a sea battle. Excavations have shown that the sculpture was placed alighting on a flagship, which was set in the ground in such a way that it appeared to float.

NYX

Nyx was female personification of night but also a great cosmogonical figure, feared even by Zeus, the king of the gods, as related in Homer's *Iliad*, Book XIV.

According to Hesiod's *Theogony*, she was the daughter of Chaos and the mother of numerous primordial powers, including Sleep, Death, the Fates, Nemesis, and Old Age. The Orphic Rhapsodies made her the daughter and successor of Phanes, a creator god; she continued to advise her own successors (Uranus, her son by Phanes; Cronus, youngest son of Uranus; and Zeus) by means of her oracular gifts. Aristotle, in *Metaphysics*, Book XII, asserted that some "theologians" derive all things from night. This idea fits the theogony of Aristophanes' *Birds*. Throughout antiquity Nyx caught the imagination of poets and artists, but she was seldom worshipped.

OCEANUS

In Hesiod's *Theogony*, Oceanus was the oldest Titan, the son of Uranus (Heaven) and Gaea (Earth), the husband of the Titan Tethys, and father of 3,000 stream spirits and 3,000 ocean nymphs. In the *Iliad*, Book XIV, Oceanus is identified once as the begetter of the gods and once as the begetter of all things; although the comments were isolated, they were influential in later thinking. Oceanus also appears in Aeschylus's *Prometheus Bound*.

In art Oceanus was a common subject; he appears on the François Vase, the Gigantomachy of the altar at Pergamum, and numerous Roman sarcophagi. As a common noun, the word received almost the modern sense of ocean.

PAN

Pan was a fertility deity, more or less bestial in form. He was associated by the Romans with Faunus. Originally an Arcadian deity, his name is a Doric contraction of *paon* ("pasturer") but was commonly supposed in antiquity to be connected with pan ("all"). His father was usually said to be Hermes, but a comic invention held that he was the product of an orgy of Odysseus's wife Penelope with her many suitors.

A stone carving depicting the god Pan. Emma Manners/Shutterstock.com

ORPHEUS

Orpheus was an ancient Greek legendary hero endowed with super-human musical skills. He became the patron of a religious movement based on sacred writings said to be his own.

Traditionally, Orpheus was the son of a Muse (probably Calliope, the patron of epic poetry) and Oeagrus, a king of Thrace (other versions give Apollo). According to some legends, Apollo gave Orpheus his first lyre. Orpheus's singing and playing were so beautiful that animals and even trees and rocks moved about him in dance.

Orpheus joined the expedition of the Argonauts, saving them from the music of the Sirens by playing his own, more powerful music. On his return, he married Eurydice, who was soon killed by a snakebite. Overcome with grief, Orpheus ventured himself to the land of the dead to attempt to bring Eurydice back to life. With his singing and playing he charmed the ferryman Charon and the dog Cerberus, guardians of the River Styx. His music and grief so moved Hades, king of the underworld, that Orpheus was allowed to take Eurydice with him back to the world of life and light. Hades set one condition, however: upon leaving the land of death, both Orpheus and Eurydice were forbidden to look back. The couple climbed up toward the opening into the land of the living, and Orpheus, seeing the Sun again, turned back to share his delight with Eurydice. In that moment, she disappeared. A famous version of the story was related by Virgil in *Georgics*, Book IV.

Orpheus himself was later killed by the women of Thrace. The motive and manner of his death vary in different accounts, but the earliest known, that of Aeschylus, says that they were Maenads urged by Dionysus to tear him to pieces in a Bacchic orgy because he preferred the worship of the rival god Apollo. His head, still singing, with his lyre, floated to Lesbos, where an oracle of Orpheus was established. The head prophesied until the oracle became more famous than that of Apollo at Delphi, at which time Apollo himself bade the Orphic oracle stop. The dismembered limbs of Orpheus were gathered up and buried by the Muses. His lyre they had placed in the heavens as a constellation.

The story of Orpheus was transformed and provided with a happy ending in the medieval English romance of *Sir Orfeo*. The character of Orpheus appears in numerous works, including operas by Claudio Monteverdi (*Orfeo*, 1607), Christoph Gluck (*Orfeo ed Euridice*, 1762), and Jacques Offenbach (*Orpheus in the Underworld*, 1858); Jean Cocteau's drama (1926) and film (1949) *Orphée*; and Brazilian director Marcel Camus's film *Black Orpheus* (1959).

A mystery religion based on the teachings and songs of Orpheus is thought to have eventually arisen in ancient Greece, although no coherent description of such a religion can be constructed from historical evidence. Most scholars agree that by the 5th century BCE there was at least an Orphic movement, with traveling priests who offered teaching and initiation, based on a body of legend and doctrine said to have been founded by Orpheus. Part of the Orphic ritual is thought to have involved the mimed or actual dismemberment of an individual representing the god Dionysus, who was then seen to be reborn. Orphic eschatology laid great stress on rewards and punishment after bodily death, the soul then being freed to achieve its true life.

Plutarch wrote that during the reign of Tiberius the crew of a ship sailing near Greece heard a voice calling out, "The great Pan is dead." Christians took this episode to be simultaneous with the death of Christ.

Pan was generally represented as a vigorous and lustful figure having the horns, legs, and ears of a goat; in later art the human parts of his form were much more emphasized. He haunted the high hills, and his chief concern was with flocks and herds, not with agriculture; hence he can make humans, like cattle, stampede in "panic" terror. Like a shepherd, he was a piper and he rested at noon. Pan was insignificant in literature, aside from Hellenistic bucolic, but he was a very common subject in ancient art. His rough figure was antithetical to, for example, that of Apollo, who represented culture and sophistication.

PANDORA

In Greek mythology, Pandora was the first woman. According to Hesiod's *Theogony*, after Prometheus, a fire god and divine trickster, had stolen fire from heaven and bestowed it upon mortals, Zeus, the king of the gods, determined to counteract this blessing. He

A later depiction of Pandora opening what came to be informally known as "Pandora's box." Photos.com/Thinkstock

accordingly commissioned Hephaestus (a god of fire and patron of craftsmen) to fashion a woman out of earth, upon whom the gods bestowed their choicest gifts. In Hesiod's *Works and Days*, Pandora had a jar containing all manner of misery and evil. Zeus sent her to Epimetheus, who forgot the warning of his brother Prometheus and made Pandora his wife. She afterward opened the jar, from which the evils flew out over the Earth. Hope alone remained inside, the lid having been shut down before she could escape. In a later story the jar contained not evils but blessings, which would have been preserved for the human race had they not been lost through the opening of the jar out of curiosity. Pandora's jar became a box in the 16th century, when the Renaissance humanist Desiderius Erasmus either mistranslated the Greek or confused the vessel with the box in the story of Cupid and Psyche.

PERSEPHONE

Persephone was the daughter of Zeus, the chief god, and Demeter, the goddess of agriculture; she was the wife of Hades, king of the underworld. In the Homeric "Hymn to Demeter," the story is told of how Persephone was gathering flowers in the Vale of Nysa when she was seized by Hades and removed to the underworld. Upon learning of the abduction, her mother, Demeter, in her misery, became unconcerned with the harvest or the fruitfulness of the Earth, so that widespread famine ensued. Zeus therefore intervened, commanding Hades to release Persephone to her mother. Because Persephone had eaten a single pomegranate seed in the underworld, she could not be completely freed but had to remain one-third of the year with Hades, spending

First-century-BCE statue of the goddess Persephone. DEA/G. Dagli Orti/De Agostini/Getty Images

the other two-thirds with her mother. The story that Persephone spent four months of each year in the underworld was no doubt meant to account for the barren appearance of Greek fields in full summer (after harvest), before their revival in the autumn rains, when they are plowed and sown.

PHOEBE

Phoebe was a Titan, daughter of Uranus (Sky) and Gaea (Earth). By the Titan Coeus she was the mother of Leto and grandmother of Apollo and Artemis. She was also the mother of Asteria and Hecate. The family relationships were described by Hesiod (*Theogony*). Her epithet was Gold-Crowned, but her name, like Apollo's forename Phoebus, signified brightness. In Aeschylus's *Eumenides* (458 BCE) she is said to have given Apollo the rite of his oracle in Delphi. In later mythology she was identified with the moon, as were Artemis and her Roman counterpart Diana.

Sculpture of the goddess Hecate, daughter of Phoebe. Time & Life Pictures/ Getty Images

POLYHYMNIA

Polyhymnia was one of the nine Muses, patron of dancing or geometry. She was said in some legends to have been the mother of Triptolemus, the first priest of Demeter and the inventor of agriculture, by Cheimarrhus, son of Ares, god of war, or by Celeus, king of Eleusis. In other versions, she was the mother of Orpheus, the legendary lyre-playing hero, or of Eros, the god of love.

POSEIDON

Poseidon was the god of the sea (and of water generally), earthquakes, and horses. He is distinguished from Pontus, the personification of the sea and the oldest Greek divinity of the waters. The name Poseidon means either "husband of the Earth" or "lord of the Earth." Traditionally, he was a son of Cronus (the youngest of the 12 Titans) and of Cronus's sister and consort Rhea, a fertility goddess. Poseidon was a brother of Zeus, the sky god and chief deity of ancient Greece, and of Hades, god of the underworld. When the three brothers deposed their father, the kingdom of the sea fell by lot to Poseidon. His weapon and main symbol was the trident, perhaps once a fish spear. According to the Greek poet Hesiod, Poseidon's trident, like Zeus's thunderbolt and Hades' helmet, was fashioned by the three Cyclopes.

As the god of earthquakes, Poseidon was also connected to dry land, and many of his oldest places of worship in Greece were inland, though these were sometimes centred on pools and streams or otherwise associated with water. In this aspect, he was known as *enosichthon* and *ennosigaios* ("earth-shaker") and was worshipped as *asphalios* ("stabilizer"). As the god of horses, Poseidon is thought likely to have been introduced to Greece by the earliest Hellenes, who also introduced the first horses to the country about the 2nd century BCE. Poseidon himself fathered many horses, best known of which was the winged horse Pegasus by the Gorgon Medusa.

Depiction on a kylix, or drinking cup, of Poseidon fighting Polybotes, a giant and son of Gaea. Universal Images Group/Getty Image

Poseidon came into conflict with a variety of figures in land disputes. Notable among these was a contest for sovereignty over Attica, which he lost to the goddess Athena. Despite losing, Poseidon was also worshipped there, particularly at Colonus (as *hippios*, "of horses").

Poseidon's offspring were myriad. He was the father of Pelias and Neleus by Tyro, the daughter of Salmoneus,

104

and thus became the divine ancestor of the royal families of Thessaly and Messenia. Many of his sons became rulers in other parts of the ancient Greek world. Otherwise he had many monstrous offspring, including giants and savage creatures, such as Orion, Antaeus, and Polyphemus. Progenitor of many, with several consorts, Poseidon also was married to the Oceanid Amphitrite, with whom he also had multiple offspring, including the sea creature Triton.

The chief festival in Poseidon's honour was the Isthmia, the scene of famous athletic contests (including horse races), celebrated in alternate years near the Isthmus of Corinth. His character as a sea god eventually became his most prominent in art, and he was represented with the attributes of the trident, the dolphin, and the tuna. The Romans, ignoring his other aspects, identified him with Neptune as sea god.

PROMETHEUS

Prometheus was one of the Titans, the supreme trickster, and a god of fire. His intellectual side was emphasized by the apparent meaning of his name, Forethinker. In common belief he developed into a master craftsman, and in this connection he was associated with fire and the creation of mortals.

The Greek poet Hesiod related two principal legends concerning Prometheus. The first is that Zeus, the chief god, who had been tricked by Prometheus into accepting the bones and fat of sacrifice instead of the meat, hid fire from mortals. Prometheus, however, stole it and returned it to Earth once again. As the price of fire, and as punishment for humankind in general, Zeus created the woman Pandora and sent her down to Epimetheus (Hindsight), who, though warned by Prometheus, married her. Pandora took the great lid off the jar she carried, and evils, hard work, and disease flew out to plague humanity. Hope alone remained within.

Hesiod relates in his other tale that, as vengeance on Prometheus, Zeus had him nailed to a mountain in the Caucasus and sent an eagle to eat his immortal liver, which constantly replenished itself; Prometheus was depicted in *Prometheus Bound* by Aeschylus, who made him not only the bringer of fire and civilization to mortals but also their preserver, giving them all the arts and sciences as well as the means of survival.

The god Prometheus carrying fire. The Bridgeman Art Library/Getty Images

RHEA

Rhea was an ancient goddess, probably pre-Hellenic in origin, who was worshipped sporadically throughout the Greek world. She was associated with fruitfulness and had affinities with Gaea (Earth) and the Great Mother of the Gods (also called Cybele). A daughter of Uranus (Heaven) and Gaea, she married her brother Cronus, who, warned that one of his children would be fated to overthrow him, swallowed his children Hestia, Demeter, Hera, Hades, and Poseidon soon after they were born. After his birth Rhea concealed Zeus in a cave on Mount Dicte in Crete and gave Cronus a stone wrapped in swaddling clothes. This he swallowed in the belief that it was Zeus. Subsequently, Cronus was vanquished by Zeus and was forced to disgorge the swallowed children.

SELENE

Selene was the personification of the moon as a goddess. She was worshipped at the new and full moons. According to Hesiod's *Theogony*, her parents were the Titans Hyperion and Theia; her brother was Helios, the sun god (sometimes called her father); her sister was Eos (Dawn). In the Homeric "Hymn to Selene," she bears the beautiful Pandeic to Zeus, while Alcman says they are the parents of Herse, the dew. She is often linked with Endymion, whom she loved and whom Zeus cast into eternal sleep in a cave on Mount Latmus; there, Selene visited him and became the mother of 50 daughters. In another story she was loved by Pan. By the 5th century BCE Selene was sometimes identified with Artemis, or Phoebe, "the bright one." She was usually represented as a woman with the moon (often in crescent form) on her head and driving a two-horse chariot. As Luna, she had temples at Rome on the Aventine and Palatine hills.

TERPSICHORE

Terpsichore was one of the nine Muses, patron of lyric poetry and dancing (in some versions, flute playing). She is perhaps the most widely known of the Muses, her name having entered general English as the adjective "terpsichorean" ("pertaining to dancing"). In some accounts she was the mother of the half-bird, half-woman Sirens, whose father was the sea god Achelous or the river god Phorcys.

THE FATES

In Greek and Roman mythology, the Fates were any of three goddesses who determined human destinies, and in particular the span of a person's life and his allotment of misery and suffering. Homer speaks of Fate (*moira*) in the singular as an impersonal power and sometimes makes its functions interchangeable with those of the Olympian gods. From the time of the poet Hesiod (8th century BCE) on, however, the Fates were personified as three very old women who spin the threads of human destiny. Their names were Clotho (Spinner), Lachesis (Allotter), and Atropos (Inflexible). Clotho spun the "thread" of human fate, Lachesis dispensed it, and Atropos cut the thread (thus determining the individual's moment of death). The Romans identified the Parcae, originally personifications of childbirth, with the three Greek Fates. The Roman goddesses were named Nona, Decuma, and Morta.

THALIA

Thalia was one of the nine Muses, patron of comedy; also, according to the Greek poet Hesiod, a Grace (one of a group of goddesses of fertility). She is the mother of the Corybantes, celebrants of the Great Mother of the Gods, Cybele, the father being Apollo, a god related to music and dance. In her hands she carried the comic mask and the shepherd's staff.

Thanatos

Thanatos was the personification of death. Thanatos was the son of Nyx, the goddess of night, and the brother of Hypnos, the god of sleep. He appeared to humans to carry them off to the underworld when the time allotted to them by the Fates had expired. Thanatos was once defeated by the warrior Heracles, who wrestled him to save the life of Alcestis, the wife of Admetus, and he was tricked by Sisyphus, the king of Corinth, who wanted a second chance at life.

Painting depicting Sisyphus, located in the Museo del Prado in Madrid, Spain. Album/Oronoz/Album/SuperStock

THEMIS

Themis was the personification of justice, goddess of wisdom and good counsel, and the interpreter of the gods' will. According to Hesiod's *Theogony*, she was the daughter of Uranus (Heaven) and Gaea (Earth), although at times she was apparently identified with Gaea, as in Aeschylus's *Eumenides* and *Prometheus Bound*. In Hesiod she is Zeus's second consort and by him the mother of the Horae, the Moirai, and, in some traditions, the Hesperides.

On Olympus, Themis maintained order and supervised the ceremonial. She was a giver of oracles; Aeschylus relates in *Eumenides* that she once owned the oracle at Delphi but later gave it to Apollo. In the lost epic *Cypria*, she plans the Trojan War with Zeus to remedy overpopulation.

The cult of Themis was widespread in Greece. She was often represented as a woman of sober appearance carrying a pair of scales.

Themis with scales, sculpture at Chuo University, Tokyo. Lucas

NYMPHS

In ancient Greek mythology, nymphs were any of a large class of inferior female divinities. The nymphs were usually associated with fertile, growing things, such as trees, or with water. They were not immortal but were extremely long-lived and were on the whole kindly disposed toward men. They were distinguished according to the sphere of nature with which they were connected. The Oceanids, for example, were sea nymphs; the Nereids inhabited both saltwater and freshwater; the Naiads presided over springs, rivers, and lakes. The Oreads (*oros*, "mountain") were nymphs of mountains and grottoes; the Napaeae (*nape*, "dell") and the Alseids (*alsos*, "grove") were nymphs of glens and groves; the Dryads or Hamadryads presided over forests and trees.

Italy had native divinities of springs and streams and water goddesses (called Lymphae) with whom the Greek nymphs tended to become identified.

TYCHE

Tyche was the goddess of chance, with whom the Roman Fortuna was later identified; a capricious dispenser of good and ill fortune. The Greek poet Hesiod called her the daughter of the Titan Oceanus and his consort Tethys; other writers attributed her fatherhood to Zeus, the supreme god. She was also associated with the more beneficent Agathos Daimon, a good spirit, protective of individuals and families, and with Nemesis, who, as an abstraction, represented punishment of over-prosperous man and so was believed to act as a moderating influence. She was often shown winged, wearing a crown, and bearing a sceptre and cornucopia; but she also appeared blindfolded and with various devices signifying uncertainty and risk. Among her monuments was a temple at Argos, where the legendary Palamedes is said to have dedicated to her the first set of dice, which he is supposed to have invented.

URANIA

U rania, meaning "heavenly," was one of the nine Muses, patron of astronomy. In some accounts she was the mother of Linus the musician (in other versions, his mother is the Muse Calliope); the father was either Hermes or Amphimarus, son of Poseidon. Urania was also occasionally used as a byname for Aphrodite. Her attributes were the globe and compass.

URANUS

U ranus was the personification of heaven. According to Hesiod's *Theogony*, Gaea (Earth), emerging from primeval Chaos, produced Uranus, the Mountains, and the Sea. From Gaea's subsequent union with Uranus were born the Titans, the Cyclopes, and the Hecatoncheires.

Uranus hated his offspring and hid them in Gaea's body. She appealed to them for vengeance, but Cronus (a Titan) alone responded. With the harpe (a scimitar) he removed Uranus's genitals as he approached Gaea. From the drops of Uranus's blood that fell on her were born the Furies, the Giants, and the Meliai (ash-tree nymphs). The severed genitals floated on the sea, producing a white foam, from which sprang the goddess of love, Aphrodite. Cronus by his action had separated Heaven and Earth. Uranus also had other consorts: Hestia, Nyx, Hemera, and Clymene.

There was no cult of Uranus in classical Greece. This circumstance, together with the story's resemblance to Asian legends, suggests pre-Greek origins. The use of the harpe points to an Asian source, and the story bears a close resemblance to the Hittite myth of Kumarbi.

THE GRACES

The Graces were any of a group of goddesses of fertility. The name refers to the "pleasing" or "charming" appearance of a fertile field or garden. The number of Graces varied in different legends, but usually there were three: Aglaia (Brightness), Euphrosyne (Joyfulness), and Thalia (Bloom). They are said to be daughters of Zeus and Hera (or Eurynome, daughter of Oceanus) or of Helios and Aegle, a daughter of Zeus. Frequently the Graces were taken as goddesses of charm or beauty in general and hence were associated with Aphrodite, the goddess of love; Peitho, her attendant; and Hermes, a fertility and messenger god. In works of art they were represented in early times draped, later as nude female figures. Their chief cult centres were at Orchomenus in Boeotia, Athens, Sparta, and Paphos. The singular Gratia or Charis is sometimes used to denote the personification of Grace and Beauty.

ZEUS

Zeus was the chief deity of the pantheon, a sky and weather god who was identical with the Roman god Jupiter. His name clearly comes from that of the sky god Dyaus of the ancient Hindu Rigveda. Zeus was regarded as the sender of thunder and lightning, rain, and winds, and his traditional weapon was the thunderbolt. He was called the father (i.e., the ruler and protector) of both gods and men.

According to a Cretan myth that was later adopted by the Greeks, Cronus, king of the Titans, upon learning that one of his children was fated to dethrone him, swallowed his children as soon as they were born. But Rhea, his wife, saved the infant Zeus by substituting a stone wrapped in swaddling clothes for Cronus to swallow and hiding Zeus in a cave on Crete. There he was nursed by the nymph (or female goat) Amalthaea and guarded by the Curetes (young warriors), who clashed their weapons to disguise the baby's cries. After Zeus grew to manhood he led a revolt against the Titans and succeeded in dethroning Cronus, perhaps with the assistance of his brothers Hades and Poseidon, with whom he then divided dominion over the world.

As ruler of heaven Zeus led the gods to victory against the Giants (offspring of Gaea and Tartarus) and successfully crushed several revolts against him by his fellow gods. According to the Greek poet Homer, heaven was located on the summit of Olympus, the highest mountain in Greece and the logical home for a weather god. The other members of the pantheon resided there with Zeus

Bronze head of Zeus, from Olympia, Greece. DEA/G. Dagli Orti/De Agostini/Getty Images

and were subject to his will. From his exalted position atop Mount Olympus Zeus was thought to omnisciently observe the affairs of men, seeing everything, governing all, and rewarding good conduct and punishing evil. Besides dispensing justice—he had a strong connection with his daughter Dike (Justice)—Zeus was the protector of cities, the home, property, strangers, guests, and supplicants.

Zeus was well known for his amorousness—a source of perpetual discord with his wife, Hera—and he had many love affairs with both mortal and immortal women. In order to achieve his amorous designs, Zeus frequently assumed animal forms, such as that of a cuckoo when he ravished Hera, a swan when he ravished Leda, or a bull when he carried off Europa. Notable among his offspring were the twins Apollo and Artemis, by the Titaness Leto; Helen and the Dioscuri, by Leda of Sparta; Persephone, by the goddess Demeter; Athena, born from his head after he had swallowed the Titaness Metis; Hephaestus, Hebe, Ares, and Eileithyia, by his wife, Hera; Dionysus, by the goddess Semele; and many others.

Though regarded by Greek religionists everywhere as omnipotent and the head of the pantheon, Zeus's very universality tended to reduce his importance compared to that of powerful local divinities like Athena and Hera. Although statues of Zeus Herkeios (Guardian of the House) and altars of Zeus Xenios (Hospitable) graced the forecourts of houses, and though his mountaintop shrines were visited by pilgrims, Zeus did not have a temple at Athens until the late 6th century BCE, and even his temple at Olympia postdated that of Hera.

In art Zeus was represented as a bearded, dignified, and mature man of stalwart build; his most prominent symbols were the thunderbolt and the eagle.

GLOSSARY

allegory The expression by means of symbolic fictional figures and actions of truths or generalizations about human existence.

antiquarian Of or relating to the study of antiquities, or relics from the ancient past.

Archaic Of or belonging to the early or formative phases of a culture or a period of artistic development.

bowdlerize To modify by abridging, simplifying, or distorting in style or content.

Classical Of or relating to the ancient Greek and Roman world and especially to its literature, art, architecture, or ideals.

cosmogonical Of or relating to the creation or origin of the world or universe.

etiologic Assigning or seeking to assign a cause.

harangue A ranting speech or writing.

Hellenistic Of or relating to Greek history, culture, or art after Alexander the Great.

intercalate To insert between or among existing elements or layers.

internecine Of, relating to, or involving conflict within a group.

lyric Expressing direct usually intense personal emotion especially in a manner suggestive of song, as in lyric poetry.

Minoan Of or relating to a Bronze Age culture of Crete that flourished about 3000 BCE–1100 BCE.

Mycenaean Characteristic of the Bronze Age Mycenaean culture of the eastern Mediterranean area.

Olympian One of the ancient Greek deities dwelling on Olympus.

patronymic A name derived from that of the father or a paternal ancestor usually by the addition of an affix.

personification Attribution of personal qualities, especially representation of a thing or abstraction as a person or by the human form.

substratum An underlying support.

temenos A parcel of ground surrounding a temple or sacred place.

tragedian A writer of tragedies.

FOR FURTHER READING

Bryant, Megan E. *Oh My Gods!: A Look-It-Up Guide to the Gods of Mythology*. New York, NY: Scholastic, 2010.

Campbell, Joseph. *The Hero with a Thousand Faces*. Princeton, NJ: Princeton University Press, 1972.

Campbell, Joseph, Bill D. Moyers, and Betty S. Flowers. *The Power of Myth*. New York, NY: Anchor, 1991.

Cotterell, Arthur. *The Illustrated Guide to the Mythology of the World: Ancient Greek, Roman, Egyptian, Norse, Chinese, Indian and Japanese*. London, England: Lorenz, 2011.

Green, Roger Lancelyn, Alan Langford, and Rick Riordan. *Tales of the Greek Heroes*. London, England: Puffin, 2009.

Hamilton, Edith, and Christopher Wormell. *Mythology*. New York, NY: Back Bay, 2011.

Hesiod, Theognis, and Dorothea Wender, trans. *Theogony, Works and Days, and Elegies*. London, England: Penguin, 2004.

Homer, Richmond Lattimore, and Richard P. Martin. *The Iliad of Homer*. Chicago, IL: University of Chicago, 2011.

Homer, Robert Fagles, trans., and Bernard Knox, ed. *The Odyssey*. New York, NY: Viking, 2006.

Leeming, David Adams. *The Oxford Companion to World Mythology*. Oxford, England: Oxford University Press, 2005.

Napoli, Donna Jo, and Christina Balit. *Treasury of Greek Mythology: Classic Stories of Gods, Goddesses, Heroes & Monsters*. Washington, DC: National Geographic Society, 2011.

Otfinoski, Steven. *All in the Family: A Look-It-Up Guide to the In-laws, Outlaws, and Offspring of Mythology*. New York, NY: F. Watts/Scholastic, 2010.

INDEX

A

Achilles, 21, 62
Adonis, 28, 48, 49
Aphrodite, 19, 20, 27–29, 34, 35,
    48, 49, 63, 64, 72, 117, 118, 119
Apollo, 13, 19, 20, 21, 24, 30–33,
    36, 39, 48, 52, 78, 81, 94, 95,
    100, 111, 114, 122
Ares, 27, 34–35, 43, 63, 100, 122
Argonauts, 14, 20, 21, 94
Arion, 22
Artemis, 32, 36–38, 41, 88, 100,
    109, 122
Asclepius, 20, 32, 39, 52, 70, 82
Athena, 13, 19, 20, 24, 25, 41–44,
    60, 74, 90, 104, 122
Atlas, 45

B

bacchantes, 57, 59, 94

C

Calliope, 46, 47, 48, 94, 117
Canathus, 13
Cassandra, 33
Centaurs, 24, 25, 29, 39

Cerberus, 68, 76, 94
Charon, 20, 94
Clio, 46, 47, 48
Cronus, 16, 18, 27, 50, 66, 68, 73,
    81, 91, 103, 108, 118, 120
Curetes, 13, 120
Cyclops, 30, 52, 103, 118

D

Daphne, 24, 32
Deimos, 34, 35
Delphi, 19, 28, 32, 46, 55, 70, 94,
    100, 114
Demeter, 19, 21, 22, 50, 53–56, 68,
    98, 102, 108, 122
Dionysus, 13, 19, 29, 57–60, 72,
    94, 95, 122
Dioscuri, 21
divination, 70, 78

E

Echo, 59
Eos, 61–62, 109
Erato, 46, 47
Eros, 27, 28, 29, 35, 63–64, 102
Europa, 22, 25

Eurydice, 15, 94
Euterpe, 46, 47, 65

F

Fates, 91, 110, 112
Four Ages of myth, 14, 17–18
Furies, 65, 68, 118

G

Gaea, 16, 32, 50, 52, 53, 65, 66–67,
    86, 92, 100, 108, 114, 118, 120
Graces, 28, 111, 119

H

Hades, 15, 17, 21, 22, 50, 53, 68, 78,
    94, 98, 103, 108, 120
Harmonia, 27, 35
Hebe, 71, 122
Helios, 17, 24, 61, 62, 108, 119
Hephaestus, 27, 52, 72, 97, 122
Hera, 13, 20, 22, 34, 50, 56, 57, 59,
    60, 68, 71, 72, 73–74, 75, 84,
    108, 119, 122
Heracles, 14, 15, 20, 21, 25, 35, 43, 71,
    75–77, 85
Hermes, 19, 23, 39, 57, 63, 78–80,
    81, 90, 93, 117, 119
Hesiod, 16, 17, 18, 19, 20, 45, 46, 48,
    52, 61, 63, 65, 86, 91, 96, 97,
    100, 103, 106, 109, 110, 111,
    114, 116, 118
Hestia, 50, 68, 81, 108, 118
Homer, 19, 20, 21, 27, 34, 36, 38, 39,
    41, 43, 45, 46, 52, 53, 62, 71, 84,
    91, 98, 109, 120
Hyacinthus, 21, 24, 49

Hygieia, 82
Hylas, 20
Hypnos, 84, 87, 112

I

Icarus, 24, 25
Iliad, 39, 41, 43, 84, 91, 92
incubation, 70

L

Leda, 22, 25, 88, 122
Leto, 24, 30, 36, 100, 122
literature, representation of
    myths in, 26

M

Medusa, 103
Melpomene, 46, 47, 85
Metis, 41, 122
Midas, 24
Minotaur, 14, 15
Mnemosyne, 46, 86
Morpheus, 84, 87
Muses, 20, 46–47, 48, 49, 65,
    85, 86, 94, 102, 110, 111, 117
myth, forms of
    folktales, 14–15
    legends, 14
    religious myths, 13–14
myths, types of
    of ages of the world, 17–19
    of the gods, 19–20, 23
    of fantastical lands or
        creatures, 24
    of heroes, 20–21
    of human hubris, 23–24

of metamorphoses, 22–23, 24
of seasons, 21–22

N

Naiads, 20, 36, 115
Narcissus, 24, 59
Nemesis, 88, 91, 116
Nike, 89–90
Niobe, 24
nymphs, 20, 24, 36, 59, 115, 118
Nyx, 65, 84, 88, 91, 118

O

Oceanus, 92, 116, 119
Odysseus, 15, 93
Odyssey, 21, 27, 43, 45, 46, 52, 78
Olympus, 13, 30, 46, 114, 120, 122
Oread, 59, 115
Orpheus, 15, 46, 47, 48, 59,
    94–95, 102

P

Pan, 24, 59, 93, 95, 78, 109
Pandora, 16, 18, 96–97, 106
Paris, 19
Pegasus, 22, 103
Persephone, 21, 22, 48, 53, 60,
    98–99, 122
Perseus, 21, 25, 43, 45, 75
Phaethon, 24
Phobos, 27, 34, 35
Phoebe, 100, 109
Polyhymnia, 46, 47, 102
Poseidon, 19, 22, 50, 55, 68, 81,
    103–105, 108, 117, 120
Prometheus, 16, 19, 45, 96, 97, 106

R

Rhea, 50, 53, 68, 73, 81, 103,
    108, 120

S

Satyrs, 20, 24
Selene, 61, 109
Semele, 57, 60, 122
sileni, 20, 60
Sirens, 25, 85, 94, 110
Styx, River, 89, 94

T

temples and shrines, 70
Terpsichore, 46, 47, 110
Thalia, 46, 47, 111
Thamyris, 20
Thanatos, 84, 112
Themis, 114
Theogony, 16, 45, 48, 61, 63, 91,
    96, 100, 109, 114, 118
Theseus, 15, 20, 25
Titans, 16, 45, 50, 60, 61, 67,
    68, 73, 86, 92, 100, 103,
    106, 109, 116, 118, 120, 122
Tithonus, 62
Trojan War, 14, 20, 48, 65, 84, 114
Troy, 14, 62
Tyche, 116

U

Urania, 46, 47, 52, 117
Uranus, 16, 27, 50, 65, 66, 86, 91,
    92, 100, 108, 114, 118

V

Virgil, 19, 62, 94
visual art, representation of
    myths in, 25

W

Works and Days, 17, 97

Z

Zeus, 13, 16, 18, 21, 22, 23, 25, 27,
    30, 34, 36, 39, 41, 43, 45, 46,
    48, 50, 52, 53, 57, 59,   60, 62,
    63, 67, 68, 71, 72, 75, 78, 81,
    84, 86, 88, 90, 91, 96, 97, 98,
    103, 106, 108, 109, 114, 116,
    119, 120–122